20TH CENTURY ROCK AND ROLL

PUNK

Dave Thompson

WATCH FOR THE REST OF THE SERIES

A GUIDE TO THE ARTISTS WHO MADE THE CENTURY'S GREATEST ROCK MUSIC

20th CENTURY ROCK AND ROLL

A COLLECTOR'S GUIDE PUBLISHING SERIES

Psychedelia	ISBN 1-896522-40-8
Alternative Music	ISBN 1-896522-19-X
Progressive Rock	ISBN 1-896522-20-3
Heavy Metal	ISBN 1-896522-47-5
Pop Music	ISBN 1-896522-25-4
Punk Rock	ISBN 1-896522-27-0
Glam Rock	ISBN 1-896522-26-2
Women In Rock	ISBN 1-896522-29-7

For ordering information see our web site at
www.cgpublishing.com

All rights reserved under article two of the Berne Copyright Convention (1971).
No part of this book may be reproduced or transmitted in any form or by any means,
electronic or mechanical, including photocopying, recording, or by any information storage
and retrieval system without permission in writing from the publisher.
We acknowledge the financial support of the Government of Canada through
the Book Publishing Industry Development Program for our publishing activities.
Published by Collector's Guide Publishing Inc., Box 62034, Burlington, Ontario, Canada, L7R 4K2
Printed and bound in Canada
20th Century Rock and Roll - Punk
by Dave Thompson
ISBN 1-896522-27-0

20TH CENTURY ROCK AND ROLL
PUNK

Dave Thompson

Table Of Contents

Table Of Contents

Acknowledgements

Much of the information in this book was drawn from my own interviews and conversations with band members over the years — thanks here, then, to (in order of appearance): John Lydon, Glen Matlock, Brian James, Rat Scabies, Knox, Pete Shelley, Steve Diggle, Siouxsie Sioux, Steve Severin, Budgie, Gaye Advert, TV Smith, Howard Pickup, Tim Cross, Kid Reid, Gene October, James Stevenson, Eddie Stanton, Billy Idol, Tony James, John Towe, Jimmy Pursey, Dave Treganna, Mick Rossi, Ari Upp, Colin Newman, Poly Styrene, Elvis Costello, Ian Dury, Rod Latter, Alan Lee Shaw, Andy Ellison, Martin Gordon, Chris Townson, Tom Robinson, Dolphin Taylor, Hugh Cornwell, Dave Sinclair, Bob Geldof, Jon Moss, Shane MacGowan, Rikki Sylvan, Vince Seggs, Dave Ruffy, Charlie Harper, Nicky Garratt, Alvin Gibbs, Beki Bondage.

Special thanks to Jo-Ann Greene for The Sex Pistols, Tim Smith for the Roxy, all at Captain Oi! and Overground, and to Mike Scharman for filling in the gaps.

Before We Start . . .

This is not a book about the 40 greatest punk bands, although it could be seen as such.

Neither is it a book about the 40 bands who, in the parlance of rock archaeology, "meant the most" — although, again it could be. Rather, it's a totally subjective, if not quite random, sampling of maybe one-fiftieth of the total number of groups who flourished in the UK between 1976-79, that period which saw a massive insurgence of new bands emerge from the sprawls of town and country alike, to be bound together in the mind of the media as Punks; Punk Rockers; Satanic Anarchist Hellspawn bent on the overthrow of decent society as we know it.

Some of them might have succeeded as well.

Of course all the big boys are here. Mention punk without mention of the Pistols or The Clash or The Damned or The Adverts or Sham 69 or The Table — well, there we go . . .

But there are others who remain fresh in the mind without the benefit of bloodlust, major record deals and screaming gore-streaked headlines. Those who cut maybe one now-scratched single, maybe a few, and then vanished back into obscurity (from which, in some cases, only the odd spin on John Peel's nightly radio show had rescued them in the first place.)

Others still went largely unheard until, in recent years, their pasts were resurrected on CD compilations, cause indeed for a whole new generation to sit around scratching its collective head and saying, "hmmm, my dad never told me about that lot."

And others still meant (and mean) nothing until you glance at the names of the hopeful former members, and think, "ah, so that's where so-and-so got started." These are the bands which lie at the soul of this book, the ones who didn't get a big fat career out of rebellion and revolution (even though they may have wanted to), the ones who didn't grind around the industry ass-kissing circuit until somebody finally pinned a long service award onto their now-expiring heart, the ones who might as well never have existed for all the attention mainstream music history affords them today. There are a thousand punk encyclopedias out there that grave-rob the big boys again and again. How many deify the Shapes?

Not all of the band biographies are complete. Sad but true — with the best will in the world, few groups can ever maintain their initial power, glory and momentum once they've passed their first few years together. They implode or explode — members quit or get religion, directions change and desires mutate. Sometimes, they simply stop making decent records and turn into precisely the kind of vaudeville embarrassment they once seemed an antidote for. Either way, we stop caring.

What this book aims to do, in those instances, is pinpoint the period during which a group was at the peak of its powers — at least as far as what we understand to be "punk rock" is concerned. It's impossible, of course, to relive, or even recapture, the sensations and emotions that flooded through the music scene during those tumultuous years at the end of the 1970's. But travel in the company of the bands in this book, in the timespan of this book, and you can at least come close.

There is no attempt to analyze those sensations, however; no lofty dissertations on the Meaning Of Punk, the History Of Punk, or the underlying socio-economic factors which turned a nation of blissfully stoned ELP and Jethro Tull fans into snot-caked safety-pinned, spiky haired eco-terrorists. Punk was never about reasons, it was about action. It was never about philosophy, it was about feelings. Suffice to say that it happened. And suffice to say that for a few moments there, they really did mean it. Man.

The movement had its intellectuals, of course (all the more so after a few years had passed and everyone felt duty bound to explain why they had acted the way they did), but it also had its idiots. And while some people may truly have cared about Hannah Arendt's theory of Creative Destruction (the notion that you have to knock things down to build them back up better), far more were interested simply in the music which was doing the job. If, indeed, that is what it was doing.

What all 40 bands in this book have in common, then, is —

a) They're all either British or (in one case) Irish. After a lot of heart searching, head scratching and record playing, common sense produced a mountain of learned rock tomes, all of which insisted that 90% of the American groups that are occasionally called punk today, either hated the term or had never even heard of it until a passing Brit dropped it into a review. So, Patti Smith, Television, Talking Heads, Richard Hell . . . well, maybe someone will write an art rock book instead.

b) They may not agree with the punk terminology either. But chronology, geography, history, and convenience will not be deterred. If they weren't punks, hated punk, would rather have been Tonto's Expanding Headband than punks — then why did they make records that sounded the way they did?

c) They're good. But even more important than that, they're varied. A collection based around the 40 bands here would effectively touch every base required for a well-rounded education in the music, and an understanding as well of how (say) Elvis Costello could find himself rubbing genres with The Damned, or Ian Dury with The Boys. Chronology, geography, history, convenience . . . and attitude. And of them all, it's the attitude that matters most of all.

These 40 bands just had a lot more than most.

Contents

This book is divided into four sections: Two conforming to actual historical events / periods — those groups who, through 1975-76, created a scene large enough to stage its own festival at London's 100 Club in September 1976, and those who formed in the wake of that event to emerge more or less fully formed onto the stage of the Roxy club during January-April, 1977; And two sections adhering to vaguer concepts — existing bands who were swept into the punk / new wave movement by circumstances beyond their control; along with bands formed in the wake of the first wave, groups whose own vision of punk often had little in common with their predecessors, but whose spirit would burn brightly regardless.

⪻ Part One ⪼
– The 100 Club Festival –

Over two nights, September 20-21, 1976, the 100 Club in London staged the first ever true gathering of the clans, a Punk festival featuring the cream of existing talent — the Pistols, The Clash, Subway Sect and Siouxsie and the Banshees appeared on the first night; The Damned, Chris Spedding and The Vibrators, The Buzzcocks and French rockers Stinky Toys on the second. The place was packed.

⪻ 1 ⪼
The Sex Pistols

In 1974, Steve Jones, Paul Cook and one Warwick Nightingale were west London teenagers rehearsing together, using equipment that Jones had allegedly lifted from backstage at the Hammersmith Odeon. Searching for a benefactor, they introduced their group, the Strand (named from a Roxy Music song) to Malcolm McLaren, owner of a Kings Road, Chelsea boutique called Let It Rock.

McLaren, in turn, introduced them to Glen Matlock, a would-be bass player who worked at the store on Saturdays. With the newcomer accompanied by a keen repertoire of 60's Mod hits, the Strand sequestered themselves in the semi-derelict hole of what had been (and would again become) Hammersmith's Riverside Studios, and rehearsed.

They rehearsed through the remainder of 1974, while their mentor, McLaren, was away in New York. Nightingale quit, Jones took over on vocals, and they were still rehearsing when McLaren returned a year later with his head full of the magic he'd been a part of in the US.

He'd been working with glam rock casualties the New York Dolls, taking over their management at a time when their every other business associate had taken the first road out. The Dolls first met McLaren in summer 1973, when he and partner Viv Westwood were in town trying to shop Westwood's latest clothes designs, retro 50's chic meets A CLOCKWORK ORANGE. They never took a single order, but the Dolls were impressed and they all kept in touch.

McLaren redesigned the Dolls, dressed them as Communists and was kind of surprised that no-one took to them that much. An attempt at an American tour fizzled out in Florida, and the Dolls broke up and returned to New York in pieces. By the time McLaren rejoined them there, guitarist Johnny Thunders and drummer Jerry Nolan had already formed a new group, the Heartbreakers, and McLaren briefly tried luring their bassist, Richard Hell, away from them. When he failed he went home, back to see how the Strand were doing.

The band's name changed to match McLaren's shop. The Strand became The Sex Pistols, just as Let It Rock, erstwhile hang-out of London's Teddy Boy community (50's revivalists in Bill Haley drag) fused into the day-glo outrage of Sex. Where once had hung exquisite drapery and bootlace ties, crepe soled shoes and drainpipe pants, now all was bondage pants and nude cowboy t-shirts, enduring regular visits from the boys in blue and building a reputation for being provocatively challenging. It only followed that The Sex Pistols should adopt a similar approach.

Certainly World's End, the increasingly apposite deep Chelsea neighborhood close to one of whose corners Sex's white storefront lurked, had not seen such excitement since the halcyon days of the hippie. Just around a dog's leg corner from Sex stood Granny Takes A Trip, the boutique which was, to the Love and Peace brigade, all that McLaren's little enterprise became to their polar opposite. And even that early in the day, a visit to the Town Records store, smack between the two, felt like a time slip into no-man's-land. On your left, then, paisley and patchouli and armpit hair to the midriff . . . and on your right, it's pictures of penises and a new shirt honoring the Cambridge Rapist. There was usually a knot of disconsolate Teddy Boys around there as well, holding their cigarettes between forefinger and thumb, mouthing "be-bop" to one other by way of secret code, "Duck's Arse" hair and Edwardian threads, and just enough bottle to return to their disinherited stomping grounds, to leer in disgust at the new range of clothes. McLaren had sold them out, and the running battles between Teds and Punks that later disfigured the summer of '77 was born right there.

Despite accepting McLaren's gifts of clothing, The Sex Pistols were still a formless, image-less bunch of tosspots, yowling away with Jones on lead vocals, and McLaren behind the scenes, trying to find a new singer. But nothing worked. A visit to Glasgow introduced him to a young vocalist named Midge Ure, then plowing the local circuit with a bonny wee band called Salvation, years ahead of his transformation into the Ultravox icon of suaveness and synths. McLaren offered him a try-out with the Pistols, Ure turned him down. Salvation had just signed to Bell Records, were changing their name to Slik and were now being groomed as the next Bay City Rollers (they later had a UK No. 1 hit, *Forever And Ever*. It's still the best thing Midge ever did.)

There was a rocker kid named Dave, who looked great but wasn't much better than Jones in the tonsil department. They showed him the door.

And then there was John.

Actually, there were three Johns, who seemed to come as a package. The tall one, John Ritchie, was a Bowie freak with a ready laugh and a self-depreciating attitude which seemed to make everyone like him. His friends called him Sid to annoy him, and Vicious because he wasn't.

The middle one, John Wardle, was built like a docker, drank like a fish and seemed undecided what he wanted to be when he grew up, a sailor or a psychopath. The others called him Wobble, because he was so big and Jah because he liked reggae.

And the short one, John Lydon, had just hacked his blond hair short and green, boasted a permanent slouch and disgusting teeth and, the first time McLaren's assistant, Bernie Rhodes, saw him, he was sporting a Pink Floyd t-shirt with "I Hate" scrawled in ballpoint just above the band name. He had an attitude too, but you needed to scrape past the silence first, not sure whether it was shyness or rudeness. Then you'd touch one of the nerves which bristled so close to the surface, and the Lydon wit would stir, corrosive, cruel and cripplingly funny. He didn't have a nickname, but Steve Jones soon found one, the moment he saw Johnny's teeth. They were rotten.

The three Johns hung together wherever there was trouble, or the possibility of making some, with Sex a kind of neutral territory where they could just watch other people. They bought things there as well and McLaren, already intrigued by the misshapen Lydon, grew more enamored every time he saw him, a mutant Frankenstein in search of a Doctor to make everything better. Finally, in late August, 1975, McLaren swooped. "Can you sing?"

"No."

"Great, I want you to meet my band." He set up a meeting at seven that same evening, at the Roebuck pub. Uncertain, unwilling, Lydon mumbled and sniped, but he was as intrigued as McLaren. He had no musical talent, no musical dreams and, in an age of glam rock beauty, he made the beast look pretty. What on earth was the old man planning? Watching the spectacle develop over an uncomfortable evening with matchmaker Malcolm, Cook, Jones and Matlock were wondering the same thing.

Only half-protestingly, Lydon allowed himself to be steered back down to Sex, someone plugged in the jukebox and Alice Cooper's *School's Out* came spit-ripping out. Lydon launched into a what-the-fuck mime, and McLaren was sold. John Lydon was in the Pistols . . .

. . . but were the Pistols into John Lydon? No. They didn't even bother turning up to their first rehearsal with him, just left him waiting all night at the Crunchy Frog pub and, when Matlock called him the next day to say sorry, Lydon threatened to kill him with a hammer.

Things just went downhill from there.

The Pistols played their first live show on November 6, 1975 at St Martin's College of Art in London. Matlock was a student there and arranged for his group to open for visiting retro-rockers Bazooka Joe. In the ten minutes before the plug was pulled on them, the Pistols managed five songs, the Small Faces *Whatcha Gonna Do About It?* and the Who's *Substitute* among them. It was, all parties would ultimately agree, a fairly unspectacular debut, but clearly the Pistols had some effect. A mere two years on, Bazooka Joe vocalist Stuart Goddard re-emerged as Adam Ant.

A second Pistols' show the following night, at the Central School of Art and Design in Holborn, went better. This time, one of Matlock's friends arranged it and, without the mysterious hand of doom to kill the juice in mid-jamboree, the group actually shambled through their entire set.

More shows at London colleges followed and at each, audiences were neatly, if extremely unevenly, divided between those who loved the band and those who thought they were crap. In years to come, of course, once they realized that an early sighting of the Pistols offered some very serious bragging rights, many of the latter would change their minds. For the former, it was enough simply to change their lives.

Either way, as The Sex Pistols' reputation grew, so did the need to supplant their repertoire of covers with originals. Not that the covers remained strictly recognizable — Lydon remembers, "they wanted to do a song by the Small Faces (*Whatcha Gonna do About It?*) The lyrics went something like, 'I want you to know that I love you baby, I want you to know that I care.'" He changed it to "I want you to know that I hate you . . . ," then explained, "the exact opposite seemed to work much better."

The rough Pistols rehearsal tapes which eventually leaked onto the GREAT ROCK'N'ROLL SWINDLE soundtrack album maintain this policy of deliberately mutilating "classic" songs. One by one, the Monkees' *Steppin' Stone*, Chuck Berry's *Johnny B Goode* and the Modern Lovers' *Roadrunner* are held out as examples of typical rehearsal room-standard pop group fare, then dismantled with a barbarity which is no less effective for having patently been done for effect.

Still a long way from anarchy, vacancy and dismantling the monarchy, The Sex Pistols nevertheless understood that the best reaction they could hope for was a negative one, and they were going out of their way to court it. Their calling card was simply one of deliberate contradiction: scruffy clothes in an age when smart ones were fashionable (when was the last time Rick Wakeman went onstage in a ripped T-shirt?), short hair hacking through the rock-norm of long, and a joyous disregard for musicianship. The notion that, through all this, they would instantly connect with an army of like-minded kids was already germinating. All that was needed now was to put that manifesto into words, then set those words to a high energy tune.

From the outset, Johnny Rotten insisted he would write the group's lyrics. He was equally insistent that he wanted nothing to do with the music beyond the autocratic right of approving it. Not that the lyrics he was delivering (and had always enjoyed writing) would have suited anything but the bomb-blasted bombast to which Matlock, Jones and Cook applied them, but it was nice to think he had a choice.

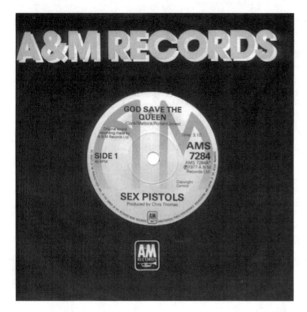

Taking the standard themes of youth disorientation, then twisting them through Rotten's own sense of sociological distortion, pretty much The Sex Pistols' entire repertoire was composed by the summer of 1976. *Seventeen, Satellite, Problems, Pretty Vacant, God Save The Queen, Anarchy In The UK* and *No Feelings.* When McLaren mentioned the Dolls too often, Rotten responded by writing *New York.* When he got sick of reading about the forthcoming Royal Jubilee, Elizabeth II's glorious 25 years on the British throne, he came up with *God Save The Queen.* And so on.

The benefits of his penmanship, of course, were two-fold, ensuring not only that the group would possess a genuinely marketable public profile by the time the media finally cottoned on to them, but also setting a standard by which any bands forming in admir/emul-ation of the Pistols could judge themselves. Anybody, after all, could change the lyrics to a famous song. But could they write one themselves that could prove just as famous? The Punk ethic of Do It Yourself was forming around the notion that if The Sex Pistols could write their own songs, anyone could. Now, the only cover that The Sex Pistols could reliably be expected to perform was *No Fun,* the anthem of utter disaffection that kicks off side two of the first Stooges album.

"I love what they did to *No Fun,*" says Iggy Pop. "It's like looking at a pile of rubbish, and knowing that you made it rubbish." In the early days, the Pistols often started their live show with it. By the end of their career, they closed with it, so the final moments of the last ever Pistols gig remain burned in rock legend forever, a croak of despair, "this is no fun . . . no fun at all."

Ah, but it was fun once.

On December 9, the Pistols played Ravensbourne Art College in front of the now-customary gaggle of disbelieving straights, and a handful of utterly entranced misfits and weirdos, for whom the Pistols' disdain not only for their audience, but for their material as well, spraypainted the entire world with a Road To Damascus-like sheen. Certainly one Simon Barker thought so, and he hastened away to tell his friends. The next time the Pistols played, their fan club was swollen by three — Steve Bailey, Sue Dallion and William

Broad, henceforth known as the Bromley Contingent, but metamorphosing also into (respectively) Steve Havoc (aka Severin) and Siouxsie of the Banshees, and Billy Idol of Generation X.

Early in 1976, McLaren pulled off the impossible, scoring his still inexperienced Pistols an opening slot at the Marquee Club on February 12. The headliners were Eddie & The Hot Rods, a group who'd cut their teeth on the pub circuit and were now showcasing for Island Records. Except it wouldn't be them who were showcased.

The New Music Express' concert review said it all: "Don't Look Over Your Shoulder, But The Sex Pistols Are Coming" and it didn't even matter if writer Neil Spencer liked the show. It was enough that he noted a thrown chair, then realized it was the "spiky haired frontman" who tossed it. He overlooked the rest of the evening's events — how there'd been a fight, and how the band did some damage to the Rods' P.A. He'd already seen enough. "The Sex Pistols are a quartet of spiky teenage misfits from the wrong end of London roads, playing 60's styled white punk rock. Punks? Bruce Springsteen and the rest of 'em would get shredded if they went up against these boys."

Two nights later, McLaren arranged for the Pistols to play a Valentine's party at artist Andrew Logan's studio, an event guaranteed to attract the cream of London's underground artist and fashion community, and raising in McLaren's mind the possibility of turning the Pistols into the new Velvet Underground or Roxy Music — acts who'd accomplished fame from similar artsy beginnings in the past.

But even with another Sex employee, the Valkyrie-esque Jordan, going topless onstage, it quickly became apparent that, in the long run, the art and fashion world weren't going to be the Pistols' ticket to success. So it was back to the colleges and the London environs and the realization that something was changing, a buzz was beginning to buzz. All the Pistols had to do was keep it humming.

Halfway through their set at the College of Higher Education in High Wycombe on February 20, Rotten's mike went out, leaving him ineffectively shouting the words to *No Fun* and waiting for something to happen. It did — a fight broke out.

Most of the audience scattered, but two young men down from Manchester, Howard Trafford and Peter Shelley, were totally enraptured — they set about arranging for the Pistols to play their hometown. Ron Watts, invited down to the show in his capacity as manager of the 100 Club in London, was similarly impressed. Immediately, he booked the group into his venue.

The Sex Pistols

The Pistols debuted at the 100 Club on March 30, 1976, collapsing into absolute chaos when Matlock decided that he'd had enough of Rotten's out of tune singing, then walked over and told him so. Rotten responded by hauling over Cook's cymbals, which naturally prompted the drummer to storm off stage and smash up a dressing room. The singer, in the meantime, left the stage and started prowling about in the crowd until McLaren — apparently with threats of imminent violence — persuaded him to return to the stage. Unfortunately, Jones took that opportunity to suddenly break all the strings on his guitar. Rotten leaped off stage again and this time, he left the club. The show was over, but the true anarchy was only just beginning.

For the crowd was going wild. Watts looked around, promptly recognized a good thing when he saw it, and vowed to have Sex Pistols back.

TV Smith, soon to form the Adverts, recalls, "it was just so great to see a band getting up and doing it, without having the proven requirements. I liked the attitude of 'like it or fuck off,' that was something that I could actually identify with. It was just so completely different . . . of course, then everyone started doing the same thing and it all settled back into nice complacent role playing."

However, the music press wasn't necessarily in agreement. Melody Maker journalist Alan Jones caught the Pistols' Nashville show on April 3, opening for the 101'ers and growled, "their dreadfully inept attempts to zero in on the kind of viciously blank intensity previously epitomized by the Stooges was rather endearing at first. The predictably moronic vocalist was cheerfully idiotic, and the guitarist, another surrogate Punk suffering from a surfeit of Sterling Morrison, played with a determined disregard for taste and intelligence." "Who's Sterling Morrison?" a bemused Jones asked afterwards.

"They were the funniest group I'd ever seen," Chris "Rat Scabies" Miller told Goldmine magazine. "They were cartoon . . . you know what it was like the first time you saw The Simpsons, the first time you saw Bart? It was a bit like that; totally larger than life, animated, horrible little gits. They were a farce. People don't think that, they think the Pistols were kind of devastating social comment. But they weren't, they were like this comedy thing, they were funny."

"At the time, everyone was into Supertramp and Eric Clapton and being able to play your instruments, and there they were . . . kids that weren't hippies with brightly colored clothes, that couldn't really play, being obnoxious to the audience. At that point in time, it was like an effrontery to all the musical taste that was going on in England. It was hysterical."

It was this suddenly sprouting audience which McLaren now wanted to capture. And the easiest way of doing that would be to open his own club. The idea of the Pistols as ring-leaders of a new scene, centered around their very own club, was one that was guaranteed to arouse press interest. Not only would it offer a haven for the increasing, and increasingly bizarre, audience which the Pistols were acquiring, it would also provide them with a back up should they be banned from any more clubs. They'd already been barred from the Marquee and the group's sets were certainly chaotic enough to assume that other venues might follow suit. And so it would prove.

He settled on El Paradise, a tiny Soho strip club, with black walls and a tiny stage that appeared somewhat bigger because of the mirrors set behind it. The night after the Nashville gig, the Pistols made their debut there, sandwiched between the strippers, only for the police to turn up and spoil the fun for everyone. McLaren started looking again. In the meantime, the Pistols set about recording their first demo, roping in grease-monkey guitar hero Chris "Motorbikin'" Spedding to oversee a three track blast of *No Feelings*, *Pretty Vacant*, and *Problems*.

Spedding explained the attraction. "They looked and sounded good — most groups are pretty boring, they weren't boring. I find it very weird all that about them not playing music. If they're notable for one thing it's that. They're always in time and in tune. I can't understand why some of the Melody Maker have chosen to attack them on the very thing that is their strength. Obviously, they've got cloth ears."

The Pistols gigged on. They stood in for the 101'ers at Walthamstow Assembly Hall, London, the original billtoppers having broken up when singer Joe Strummer left to form a new band in wide-eyed admiration of the Pistols. That group, the Clash, would play their first ever show opening for the Pistols in Sheffield in July.

They appeared at the Midsummer Music Festival Benefit with Ian Dury & The Kilburns and the Stranglers. They made two trips to Manchester, fulfilling the dreams of Shelley and Trafford, and returned to the 100 Club for what Ron Watts later called "the night that the New Wave actually started — because The Damned were on too, as support. It was their first [major] gig, but you could see they were going to make it too."

On July 18, the Pistols ran off another set of demos with their own sound engineer, Dave Goodman, producing a seven song set highlighted by the newly composed *Anarchy In The UK*, and at the end of August another attempt at launching a punks only club found them staging their own mini-festival at Islington's Screen On The Green cinema — The Clash and The Buzzcocks, formed by those same two Manchester kids who'd booked them into that city's nightlife, also appeared.

However, the stampede of record company executives which McLaren was banking on had still to materialize. Atlantic's A&R manager, Dave Dee (of Dozy, Beaky, Mick and Tich fame) shrugged, "as a musical thing I found them very unmusical — perhaps the fact that it wasn't disciplined prevented me from liking it. I could see it was valid. You can't knock anything that has an audience. It's right for now because they have an image, but I can't see it going anywhere further than where it is right now, and when you sign someone you have to think in terms of five years. We had a meeting today and we'd be interested in signing them for a single or an EP and see what happens. If their manager was sensible and didn't want the world."

Unfortunately, that was precisely what McLaren wanted, although he was also still grateful for what he could get. Through September, the Pistols' itinerary included a disco opening in Paris, a maximum security prison in Chelmsford and another trip up to Manchester, to appear on the late night TV rock show SO IT GOES. But proof that things were coalescing around The Sex Pistols' example was awaiting as well, when the group returned to London to headline the first night of the 100 Club Punk Festival.

The following week, McLaren had his first meeting with EMI A&R chief Nick Mobbs. Days later, EMI signed The Sex Pistols for a record 40,000 pound advance. A&R head Nick Mobbs told the press, "here at last is a group with a bit of guts for younger people to identify with; a group that parents actually won't tolerate. And it's not just parents that need a little shaking up; it's the music business itself."

He continued, "That's why a lot of A&R men wouldn't sign the group. They took it all too personally. But what other group at a comparable point in their career has created so much excitement both on stage and off? For me The Sex Pistols are a backlash against the 'nice little band' syndrome and the general stagnation of the music industry. They are a band who are shaking up the music business. They've got to happen. I don't think there'll be any problems with their lyrics because I've got more than a little sympathy with what they're doing. They've got to happen for all our sakes."

The Pistols celebrated the coup by heading down to Lansdowne Studios to record *Anarchy In The UK* with Dave Goodman, again, producing. The fact that EMI had made it patently clear that they wanted *Pretty Vacant* to be the first single did not enter into the group's calculations. They wanted *Anarchy* and they were going to get it, if they spent the rest of their lives trying to record it properly. The Goodman session broke down. A second attempt with EMI's own Mike Thorne at the controls went no further. Finally, the band were paired with veteran Chris Thomas, of Roxy Music and hateful Pink Floyd fame, and an acceptable take was in the can. *Anarchy In The UK* was released on November 17, 1976.

Eleven days after, the Pistols were a star attraction on television's LONDON WEEKEND SHOW, but not everybody who witnessed it was convinced by the group's growing media charms. The following day, the Lancaster town council cancelled the Pistols' show at the local Polytechnic because they didn't want "that sort of filth in the town limits." It was an astonishingly far-sighted decision.

On December 1, The Sex Pistols were asked to replace labelmates Queen on local London television's nightly TODAY magazine show, stepping in at 90 minutes notice and spending much of that time in the studios' hospitality suite. They were not drunk when they took their seats towards the end of the show, but relations between the band and host Bill Grundy had clearly not got off to the most conducive of starts.

So they bantered bad-temperedly back and forth, but it was all harmless enough until Grundy — for reasons even he was subsequently at a loss to understand — asked Rotten to repeat a "bad word" which crept out under his breath. Rotten did so, Grundy requested another . . . and the floodgates burst. Across the next 90 seconds, the Pistols unleashed more oaths than British TV had heard in one volley in 50 years and, even before Grundy bade his goodnights, the studio's switchboard was screaming its disgust.

"The Filth And The Fury!" bellowed the front page of the Daily Mirror newspaper the following morning. Four fifths of the tabloid's front page was devoted to the foul-mouths of The Sex Pistols. The remainder told readers about the 47 year old truck driver who was so concerned for the delicate sensibilities of his watching eight year old son that he physically kicked in his TV set. One still wonders what junior made of that.

Neither, however, was Mr. Truck Driver the only outraged citizen. As the day wore on, local politicians got in on the act as well, and towns which had never even heard of the TODAY show announced the cancellation of their own forthcoming Pistols' shows.

The group's tour was due to start the day after the broadcast. Instead it was in shambles. Overnight, punk rock had been transformed from a sordid undercurrent to mainstream Rock and Roll, to a foul-mouthed blasphemous vomit-caked leviathan, one which would stop at nothing until the entire nation had been corrupted. Day after day, the Pistols, The Damned, The Clash and The Heartbreakers would turn up at the town limits. Night after night it was to find that the gig was cancelled and, by the time the increasingly dispirited tour party arrived home, 16 of the scheduled 19 shows had been ignominiously canned.

The BBC banned *Anarchy* from the airwaves. EMI's own record packers refused to handle the single. At first, EMI itself stood by the band, but a meeting with

the company's shareholders showed another line of thought was beginning to creep in. While the Pistols drove from town to town only to find their next show, too, had been cancelled, EMI chairman Sir John Read announced, "The Sex Pistols have acquired a reputation for aggressive behavior which they certainly demonstrated in public. There is

The Sex Pistols

no excuse for this . . . I need hardly add that we shall do everything we can to restrain their public behavior. Our view within EMI is that we should seek to discourage records that are likely to give offense to the majority of the people . . ."

On January 4, the Pistols flew out to Amsterdam to begin a European tour. On January 6, 1977, EMI announced that the group's contract had been terminated.

Other labels showed an interest — WEA and CBS both looked closely at the combo — then withdrew, mortified by all that The Sex Pistols apparently represented. Not only that, but there was also doubt as to whether there would even be a group left to sign. Rumors that Matlock — universally regarded as the one true "musician" in the band — was on his way out had been circulating for weeks. Now they were joined by further rumors that he was to be replaced by Sid Vicious, a man whose one contribution to even the loosest definition of a musical event was hitting a rudimentary drum for Siouxsie and the Banshees at the 100 Club Punk Festival. Since then, he'd been allegedly rehearsing a new group, the Flowers Of Romance, but no-one had heard them . . . most people had never even heard of them.

Rumor, however, was correct. Matlock was out, Vicious was in. McLaren told the New Musical Express, "Glen Matlock was thrown out of The Sex Pistols, so I'm told, because he went on too long about Paul McCartney. EMI was enough. The Beatles was too much."

"It just got a bit too much in the end," Rotten agreed. "He hated our guts with a passion, really hated us. I can carry on working with someone who hates me so long as there's some kind of respect for musical ideas. He hated everything we had ever done, thought it was too strong, heavy like. He wanted it to be watered down like The Beatles. When *Anarchy* come out he hated it. We can't carry on with an arsehole like that. Sid's not so bloody serious about it. Music's meant to be fun, not like some crass music machine . . . that's what Glen wanted."

Six days after Matlock's departure, on March 9, 1977, the Pistols signed to A&M. A week later, they were dropped again, the culmination of seven days of unremitting tumult. On March 11, Rotten was arrested for possession of amphetamine sulphate. On March 12, Rotten and Jah Wobble were involved in a fight with BBC TV host Bob Harris. And on March 16, the pressing plants were told to stop production of the band's proposed new single, *God Save The Queen*.

Amid rumors of a wholesale revolt among the A&M roster — an array of talent which reached from Chris De Burgh to the Carpenters, Supertramp to Rick Wakeman — UK label head Derek Green insisted that the decision had been his alone. He signed the group on an impulse, then dropped them after much consideration. For the Pistols, the only consolation was another 35,000 pounds in the pocket.

On March 28, the Pistols played what was, in contrast with the activity of the previous year, a rare show at Notre Dame Hall in London, debuting Vicious for around 150 fans and an NBC camera crew. From there they decamped to Berlin for a few days sightseeing, then returned home to wait through a battery of increasingly absurd rumors — They were signing to CBS. They were launching their own label. They were allying themselves to the ultra-fascist National Front political party. None of them were true, all were palpably absurd. Even as the media mused on the band's next home, McLaren was finalizing an agreement with Virgin Records.

On the surface, it was a surprising move — Virgin, the label built almost exclusively on the success of Mike Oldfield's TUBULAR BELLS, the company's first ever release four years earlier, was one of the newest labels on the block, but it was also, in the public estimation, one of the most hidebound. Think of Virgin and one immediately envisioned the stoned immaculate meanderings of Gong's pothead pixies or Henry Cow's jazz-tinged noodlings . . . in other words, hippies!

But Virgin was also one of the principle distributors of reggae in the UK, both imported and homegrown, while the company's very existence, not to mention its success, was one in the eye for all the major labels who, then as much as now, seemed intent on converting the entire music industry into one vast corporate mass. Virgin may have been a bunch of hippies, but at the time they were defiant, subversive, hippies. The Pistols fit right in.

Again, *God Save The Queen* was scheduled as the group's next release, and the timing could not have been better. The Jubilee celebrations were just a heartbeat away in June, the entire country was poised on a knife-edge of patriotic fervor and delight, putting the finishing touches to what was confidently expected to be the biggest street party the country had ever seen. And here come The Sex Pistols to piss on their parade.

People saw what they wanted to see, a picture sleeve showing the Queen with a safety pin through her nose; and heard what they wanted to hear, those disgusting little monsters calling her a moron, a fascist, a non-human. And it didn't matter how often that, as the song went on, Rotten insisted "we love our Queen." Nobody was going to believe him and even fewer were going to show him any mercy.

Of course the record received a blanket radio ban, with record stores swiftly following suit. As *God Save The Queen* made its inexorable way up the chart, visitors to some of Britain's best known retail outlets were informed not only that they couldn't buy the record there, they couldn't even mention its name. The weekly chart, posted on the wall of so many stores, would bear a blank line where the Pistols' record was supposed to be, a conspiracy of ostriches that reached its peak in the week of the Jubilee celebrations themselves. In a chart calculated by record sales

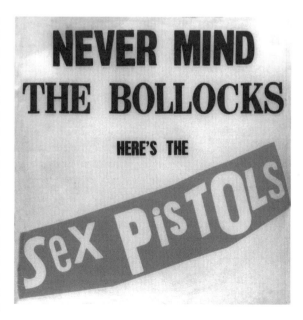

The Sex Pistols

alone, *God Save The Queen* had outsold every other single by four to one. Yet it was Rod Stewart's recounting of *I Don't Want To Talk About It* which sat at No. 1 on the chart. The Pistols, or the attendant blank line, came to a halt at No. 2.

Neither could the Pistols' own jubilee celebration be allowed to pass by unmolested. The band rented a boat, the Queen Elizabeth, to sail down the River Thames, a pleasure trip which would culminate with a short live performance as the vessel drew level with the Houses Of Parliament. Four songs into the set, the police moved in. The Queen Elizabeth was ordered to shore and the plugs were pulled. In the ensuing melee, eleven people, including McLaren, were arrested.

But the nightmare was only beginning. On June 13, the Pistols' art director, Jamie Reid, was set upon by patriotic footpads and left with a broken arm and leg. Rotten, Chris Thomas and Bill Price (manager of the recording studio where the Pistols were working) were next, attacked by five Teddy Boys in the parking lot of the Pegasus pub in Highbury, London. Thomas and Rotten were both injured, the singer had two tendons severed in his arm — the following morning, the Daily Mirror headline triumphantly trumpeted, "PUNK ROCK ROTTEN RAZORED."

Cook was attacked at Shepherd's Bush tube station by five men with knives and an iron bar. He required between 10 and 15 stitches (reports varied.) Rotten was assaulted again at a Pirates' gig at Dingwalls . . . and then the mood shifted. Regardless of the circumstances, the British have always supported the underdog, have always hated the bully. The fact that it was The Sex Pistols who were being bullied made no difference. Emerging, shocked, from a pitbull fog of Churchillian indignation, even the tabloid press suddenly realized that something had gone horribly awry. You can be vilified by the press, that's fair game, but when sticks and stones start breaking bones, that's a different matter entirely.

Consciously, the press stopped reporting on the attacks, in the apparent hope that without the lifeblood of publicity, lifeblood itself might stop being spilled. And doubtless their deliberations had some effect. But only some. Attacks on the Pistols were simply the start of it — through the summer of 1977, punks of any persuasion were fair game to the bands of brigands who would emerge from the safety of their drunken mens' clubs to chase some game down the local high street.

The violence left the punk community if not afraid, at least extremely nervous. And the Pistols, understandably, remained the most nervous of them all, which might explain why they finally chose *Pretty Vacant* as their next single, a harmless slab of rabble rousing meaningless which didn't even scare the chain stores. A video of the group performing the song was submitted to, and accepted by, TOP OF THE POPS, radio danced to the chorus of "we're so pretty" . . . less than six weeks had passed since the Jubilee and the Pistols had been forgiven everything.

Clearly confused by this new chain of events, the Pistols tried to make back lost ground. Departing Heathrow Airport for a short Scandinavian tour, the band treated the watching pressmen to a prime barrage of foul language. It barely received a mention in the following day's newspapers. Rotten agreed to a 90 minute interview on Capital Radio, playing through his favorite records, subversive dub, uncommercial Kraut rock, forgotten garage rock. He was patted on the head and congratulated for his broad taste in music.

Even the past winter's bans were now in doubt. Hatched in the white heat of the post-TODAY trauma, few of them probably stood any longer, so another bastion of the group's rebel cathedral might have fallen. The Pistols weren't in the mood to find out, though, announcing instead a "secret" British tour which would defy even the most vigilant vigilante via a variety of impenetrable pseudonyms. SPOTS, the Tax Exiles, the Special Guests, Acne Rabble, the Hamsters, "a mystery band of international repute." Round the country the Pistols went, relying on the grapevine and the curious to seek them out, then turning in some often inspired performances. They were a band, they wanted to play and finally, after all the crap of the past nine months, they were getting the chance once again.

A new single, *Holidays In The Sun*, was released, the first song recorded (or even written) by the group since Matlock's departure. It was, advance reports warned, a real shocker, a return to the pre-*Pretty Vacant* howl, a militaristic assault which compared Belsen to a holiday camp. In fact, it sounded exactly like the Jam's *In The City*, but if listeners were greeting the single with a tinge of disappointment, there was still plenty of enthusiasm for the Pistols' impending album, the beautifully titled NEVER MIND THE BOLLOCKS, HERE'S THE SEX PISTOLS. On October 24, advance orders for the record topped 125,000.

Originally scheduled for a Halloween release, BOLLOCKS was ultimately released a week early to avoid the Christmas log jam. The band themselves continued working on the album right up until the last minute. Indeed, the first pressing of the album had already been produced when the Pistols decided to add *Submission* to the running order. Hastily, the track was slammed onto a bonus 7" single (it was added to the album for subsequent pressings, rendering earlier editions a neat new collectible.)

Of course, the whole Sex Pistols business was still offensive to some people. Capitol Radio clearly agreed, banning *Holidays* on the grounds of bad taste (despite having been happily running commercials for it for several weeks) and, not to be outdone, the chain stores reinstituted their own Pistols bans on single and album alike. Portentous right wing politician Norman St. John Stevas weighed in, complaining, "[the] album has been produced deliberately to offend. It is the kind of music that is a symptom of the way society is declining. It could have a shocking effect on young people."

The Sex Pistols

For a time, Virgin pondered the possibility of simply removing any offensive tracks from the album, only to retract the suggestion when they realized that, once you'd deleted *Holidays* and *Queen* for their sentiments, the pro-life expletive laden *Bodies* for its saltiness, *Anarchy* for its politics, *EMI* for its slurs and *17* in case it upset any orphans, they'd wouldn't have much more than *Pretty Vacant* left, and the kids had already bought that once. The album went ahead as planned and with it, a fresh firestorm. You can't say "bollocks" on the radio.

"Sex Pistols In A New Four Letter Word Storm" announced The Sun newspaper, clearly losing count once it ran out of fingers on its wanking hand and, on November 5, the storm broke. That was when a Nottingham policewoman spotted posters for the album in the window of the Virgin Record store. Warning the store manager that the flagrant display of the word "bollocks" left him liable to prosecution under the Indecent Advertising Act, she asked him to remove the poster. He did, but put it up again the moment her back was turned — which meant that when she passed by again, she had no alternative but to arrest him.

The ensuing trial, ridiculous as it may seem, became a landmark case. Virgin was represented by the great John Mortimer, who immediately began researching the true meanings of the word "bollocks" and their contextual variations. What he found was fascinating — the word was first used in Anglo-Saxon texts from the first millennium, when it referred to a small ball. It reappeared in both biblical and veterinarian texts, as well as in place names, finally passing into slang during the 19th century when it was applied, of all people, to clergymen, and their propensity for talking a great deal of rubbish. A linguistics expert appearing for the defense concluded, "I would take the album title to mean 'Never Mind The Nonsense Here's The Sex Pistols'" — which, of course, was correct.

The court had no choice, telling the defendant, "much as my colleagues and I wholeheartedly deplore the vulgar exploitation of the worst instincts of human nature for the purchase of commercial profits by both you and your company, we must reluctantly find you not guilty . . ."

On November 28, McLaren announced plans for the next Pistols' tour, taking in select European destinations and, finally, the US. It would be an unconventional outing, he promised. "What I'd like to do is pick some place on the map that no-one has ever heard of before. Somewhere in Alabama or near the Mexican border and do a gig there. Even if they hate it, at least it's helping to decentralize and get away from playing New York and Los Angeles because everyone plays those shitholes." What McLaren didn't seem to understand (but the Pistols would discover) was there was good reason everyone played "those shitholes."

A handful of shows around Holland and the UK preceded their departure. So did a tussle with US immigration, who refused to issue the group with visas after discovering that all four members had criminal records, ranging from petty theft to a drug conviction (Rotten) and a weapons charge (Vicious.) The band appealed, but a show in Pittsburgh and a scheduled appearance on SATURDAY NIGHT LIVE were both lost before the tour finally got underway at the Great South East Music Hall in Atlanta, GA, on January 5, 1978.

The next ten days were, for the most part, undiluted torment, as The Sex Pistols flopped through mismatched show after mismatched show, playing punk to audiences who had come to stare at best, but usually something worse. In Memphis, the Pistols were pelted with beer cans, in Baton Rouge, coins. In San Antonio, Vicious wound up with a very photogenic bloody nose after whacking an onlooker on the head with his bass. And so on.

Rumors of band infighting, too, were seeping out, but everything seemed calm when the group reached San Francisco for the final show of the tour. Indeed, it was only in later years, after viewing the deliberately edited footage included in McLaren's posthumous GREAT ROCK'N'ROLL SWINDLE docu-drama, that the performance took on the sense of ominous fragility with which it is remembered today — Rotten asking the audience, "ever had the feeling you've been cheated?" then ending the show on his haunches, ad libbing around a broken No Fun. But it was an accurate sense regardless. While his bandmates joined McLaren in Rio De Janeiro to continue work on the SWINDLE, Rotten flew home and told the press why. He'd quit the band.

The Sex Pistols ended there and then, but their headless doppelganger carried on for another year, as the unholy hydra of Cook, Jones and Vicious saw the SWINDLE project to fruition, through a string of awkward sounding singles and a hit soundtrack album. The emergence of Rotten's Public Image Ltd, of course, banged one nail in the coffin. The death of Sid Vicious, on February 2, 1979 hammered in some more.

But it took SWINDLE itself to truly kill off the group, by replacing it with the legend which remains gospel today — how the entire thing was planned from beginning to end; how McLaren was the mastermind who forced not one, not two, but three different record labels to dole out money hand over fist; how the Pistols themselves were nothing more than a product of his imagination. And in a way they were.

But they were also a great Rock and Roll group, one of the most significant that ever lived. "Everybody foisted this myth on our shoulders," Matlock elaborated years later as the band prepared for their 1996 reunion tour, "which we never particularly wanted in the first place. That whole thing of turning the Pistols into some kind of iconic rock religion almost, is bollocks. In a way, we're kind of icon busting, and I think that's a far more healthy thing than to let it go on."

THE SEX PISTOLS DISCOGRAPHY
UK Singles
- *Anarchy In The UK / I Wanna Be Me* (EMI 2566, 1976)
- *God Save The Queen / No Feelings* (A&M AMS 7284 [withdrawn], 1977)
- *God Save The Queen / Did You No Wrong* (Virgin VS 181, 1977)
- *Pretty Vacant / No Fun* (Virgin VS 184, 1977)
- *Satellite* (one sided, free with BOLLOCKS) (Virgin DJ 24, 1977)
- *Holidays In The Sun / Satellite* (Virgin VS 191, 1977)

Post-Rotten Singles

- *No-one Is Innocent / My Way* (Virgin VS 220, 1978)
- *The Biggest Blow* / interview / *My Way* (Virgin VS 22012, 1978)
- *Something Else / Friggin' In The Riggin'* (Virgin VS 240, 1979)
- *Silly Thing / Who Killed Bambi?* (Virgin VS 256, 1979)
- *C'mon Everybody / God Save The Queen Symphony / Watcha Gonna Do About It?* (Virgin VS 272, 1979)
- *Great Rock'n'Roll Swindle / Rock Around The Clock* (Virgin VS 290, 1979)
- SID VICIOUS' HERITAGE EP: *My Way / Something Else / C'mon Everybody* (12") (Matrix Best 740.509, 1979)
- *Steppin' Stone / Pistols Propaganda* (Virgin VS 339, 1980)
- PISTOLS SIX PACK (six 45's: *Steppin' Stone / Anarchy In The UK, God Save The Queen / Pretty Vacant, Holidays In The Sun / My Way, Something Else / Silly Thing, Black Leather / Here We Go Again, C'mon Everybody / Who Killed Bambi?* (Virgin SEX 1, 1981)
- *Who Killed Bambi? / Rock Around The Clock* (Virgin VS 443, 1981)
- *Anarchy In The UK / No Fun* (Virgin VS 609, 1983)
- *Anarchy In The UK / No Fun / EMI* (Virgin VS 60912, 1983)
- *Submission / No Feelings* (Chaos DICK 1, 1985)
- *Submission / Anarchy In The UK* (12") (Chaos EXPORT 1, 1985)
- THE EARLY YEARS LIVE EP: *Anarchy In The UK / Pretty Vacant / Liar / New York* (12" blue vinyl) (Receiver REPLAY 3012, 1990)
- *Anarchy In The UK / I Wanna Be Me* (Virgin VS 1431, 1992)
- *Anarchy In The UK* (demo) / *I Wanna Be Me* (Virgin VSCDT 1431, 1992)
- *Pretty Vacant / No Feelings* (Virgin VS 1448, 1992)

Selected UK Albums

- NEVER MIND THE BOLLOCKS, HERE'S THE SEX PISTOLS (Virgin V2086, 1977)
- THE GREAT ROCK'N'ROLL SWINDLE (soundtrack) (Virgin VD 2510, 1979)
- SOME PRODUCT: CARRI ON SEX PISTOLS (Virgin VR 2, 1979)
- FLOGGING A DEAD HORSE (Virgin V2142, 1980)
- THE GREAT ROCK'N'ROLL SWINDLE (best of) (Virgin V2186, 1980)
- THE MINI ALBUM (demos) (Chaos MINI 1, 1985)
- THE ORIGINAL PISTOLS LIVE (Receiver RRLP 101, 1985)
- AFTER THE STORM (demos: split LP with New York Dolls) (Receiver RRLP 102, 1985)
- LAST SHOW ON EARTH (live) (MacDonald Bros JOCK 1, 1986)
- THE ORIGINAL PISTOLS LIVE (picture disc) (American Phono APKPD 13, 1986)
- 10TH ANNIVERSARY ALBUM (MacDonald Bros JOCKLP 3, 1986)
- THE ORIGINAL PISTOLS LIVE (Fame FA 4131491, 1986)
- THE FILTH & THE FURY (live / demos) (6 LP boxed-set) (MacDonald Bros JOCKBOX 1, 1987)
- IT SEEMED TO BE THE END UNTIL THE NEXT BEGINNING (MacDonald Bros JOCKLP 12, 1988)
- ANARCHY WORLDWIDE (live) (Specific SPAW 101, 1988)
- LIVE & LOUD (Link LINKLP 063, 1989)
- NO FUTURE UK? (live) (Receiver RRLP 117, 1989)
- THE ORIGINAL PISTOLS LIVE (Dojo DOJOLP 45, 1989)

○ PRETTY VACANT (live) (Receiver RRLP 004, 1991)
○ BETTER LIVE THAN DEAD (live) (Dojo DOJOCD 73, 1992)
○ EARLY DAZE — THE STUDIO COLLECTION (demos) (Street Link STRCD 019, 1992)
○ KISS THIS (compilation) (Virgin V2702, 1992)
○ LIVE AT CHELMSFORD PRISON (Dojo DOJOCD 66, 1993)

The Clash

When is a band not a band?

When it lives in the basement of a Paddington steak house, auditioning but seldom rehearsing, dreaming but seldom doing, writing but never recording. When it's called the London SS.

But in the course of events, the group's members — permanent and temporary — line up as a virtual Who's Who of Punk, founding relationships which, over the next two years, were to metamorphose into The Boys, The Damned and Generation X. The Punk family tree compiled by arch-archivist Pete Frame probably sums up the band's importance the best — marching towards all three of those groups, Matt Dangerfield, Brian James, Tony James, Rat Scabies and Casino Steel all passed through the band's ranks between March 1975 and January 1976 and, even though the only recorded evidence of the SS is a tape which bassist Tony James describes as "raw rock'n'roll . . . it drives like fuck", the London SS remains one of rock's most potent myths.

In March 1975, one Kelvin Colney placed an ad in Melody Maker, calling for a bass player. Among the respondents was Tony James, and while Colney (who went on to front such minor concerns as Violent Luck and the Tools) had no personal use for James' abrasive, hard rock style, he knew a man who did — his flatmate, Mick Jones. He introduced them, and for the next four months the pair worked together — Jones on rhythm guitar, James on bass — with Kings Road boutique owner Malcolm McLaren fussing around the seams, dreaming of uniting the two in one of his own greatest dreams: a Hollywood Brats reunion.

The Hollywood Brats are one of those groups that everyone knows, but few people have heard. They were Norwegian, as unlikely as that sounds, and — even more unlikely — they were the nearest thing Europe ever came to the New York Dolls, a swish, swaggering fashion statement which played fast and dirty glam rock, centered around their piece de resistance, a wasted revision of Phil Spector's *And Then He Kissed Me*.

The Brats went nowhere, but the reunion sounded like it at least had a shot, especially after a couple of ex-Brats, Casino Steele and Matt Dangerfield, dropped by to jam and rehearse. They quit after just two rehearsals (they eventually formed The Boys), though, and in July, 1975, Jones and James decided to expand their own vision, placing a second Melody Maker ad, this time calling for a guitarist and a drummer, both of whom had to adore the Dolls, Mott The Hoople, the Stones and The Stooges.

First to reply was Brian James, on the run from a growling south coast monster called, with supreme good taste and judgement, Bastard. He fit the London SS like a glove (his introduction was a phone call — "I'm a lead guitarist and I'm into the Stooges"), so much so, that even when he announced that he was off to Belgium for Bastard's farewell tour, Jones and James agreed to save him a place in the band. Then, with drummer Roland Hot installed ("probably because he had a leather jacket", says Tony James), the London SS got down to recording their demo, a couple of MC5 songs and Mick Jones' *Protex Blue*. Hot himself, in Brian James' words, would "keep the drum seat warm for three or four weeks," but time moved a lot slower in those days than it does today. Those weeks were more than enough for SS to decide they needed a new singer, and a proper manager.

One Paul Simonon answered the first call, turning up to sing an out of tune *Roadrunner*, then leaving when Mick Jones announced that he could do a better job. One of McLaren's associates, Bernie Rhodes, responded to the second and, for the next five months, the SS continued auditioning, rehearsing and writing — Brian James' *Portobello Reds*, which became The Damned's *Fish*, dates from these otherwise unheard collaborations.

But by the end of December 1975, things were still not working out. The search for a new drummer turned up Terry Chimes, who was then turned down, and Nicky "Topper" Headon, who turned the group down. There was one great drummer named Andy who passed through, "the best drummer we'd heard in our lives," marvelled Tony James. "But he couldn't accept our offer because he had a pretty serious drug problem at the time." And there was another named Chris Miller, who came to audition and left with both a new name, Rat Scabies, and a guitarist, Brian James. This pair formed The Damned soon after.

Tony James, too, was losing interest, seriously considering throwing up Rock and Roll and getting a day job instead, while Mick Jones was thinking of linking with SS rejects Terry Chimes and Paul Simonon, guitarist Keith Levine and vocalist Billy Watt, in a new act called the Psychotic Negatives.

Simonon, so unsuitable as a vocalist, turned out to be unsuitable as a bassist as well — whereas the rest of the group at least had a background in small time groups, albeit ones that knew more chords than they'd played live shows — Simonon didn't even know any chords at the time. He was so willing to learn, however, that he eventually became the only member of this embryonic band to actually survive its entire lifetime.

It was manager Bernie Rhodes who encouraged Jones to take this latest step — he alone sensed the chemistry that bound the Jones / Simonon / Chimes triumvirate together. An idealist who saw Rock and Roll as revolution as opposed to a career, Rhodes knew, even before the musicians themselves were aware of the fact, that they had the potential to bring his dream to fruition.

The name had to go. The Psychotic Negatives became the Heartdrops for a time. It was Simonon who finally came up with a new name, The Clash, after noticing how often the word appeared in newspaper headlines. It was Simonon again, out one day with Jones, who also engineered the most crucial change in the group's early line-up, when the pair met and recognized 101'ers vocalist Joe Strummer on a London street.

The 101'ers were a pub group, signed to the Chiswick indie label and awaiting the release of their debut single *Keys To Your Heart*. They were an exciting proposition, but Strummer recognized the band's limitations nevertheless. When Jones and Simonon asked him to throw it in and join the Clash, he agreed like a shot. Billy Watt was out immediately.

By June, 1976, this audacious line-up was rehearsing constantly. They already had a reasonable repertoire at their disposal — as the 101'ers' principle songwriter, Strummer in particular had a stockpile of unrecorded songs, the future anthem *Jail Guitar Doors* included. Jones' notebook, meanwhile, included *1-2 Crush On You, Deny, Bored With You, Ooh Baby Ooh, Mark Me Absent, She's Sitting At My Party* and *Protex Blue* — one of the few songs that London SS had got round to recording.

Levine and Jones together, meanwhile, penned *What's My Name*, but as the group worked through the stockpile, it became clear that few of their songs reflected the concerns which Bernie Rhodes was trying to instil in them. Love songs were out, and anti-love songs were frowned upon. If The Clash was to cut it in the new world that the prescient Rhodes foresaw (and the others could at least glimpse), they needed to write about things that they cared about, as Strummer put it, "something . . . that's real."

Bored With You offered future historians a classic example of this process in action. It was, as its title suggests, an anti-love song — "I'm so bored with you." As Strummer and Jones worked on it, however, it changed its personality completely, to the anthemic *I'm So Bored With The USA*, a commentary on what was, even then, a growing trend in British life, to think that because something was American, it was somehow more exotic.

Across the country, burger bars had stopped selling chips and offered French Fries instead. Eggs were no longer fried, they were sunny side up. Everywhere you turned, another American pseudo-miscreant was the future of Rock and Roll. Everywhere you looked, another asinine Yankee cop or comedy show was topping the ratings — and another cop (or comedy) star was topping the chart. 1976-77 saw no less a personage than Officer Starsky, David Soul, climb to No. 1 in the UK. The year before, it was Telly KOJAK Savalas. A year later it would be John WELCOME BACK KOTTER Travolta. Bored with the USA? Overwhelmed, more like.

Neither was The Clash being merely petulant when they voiced their distaste for the cultural invasion going on around them. Punk rock was a global concern, erupting like smallpox from across Europe, the US, Asia and Australia. But in each of those lands, it was also fiercely parochial, addressing the dreams, the desires and the despair of the people who were making it. And the fact that Rock and Roll itself had become all but an American ballgame only exacerbated the need to render the music into distinctly nationalistic terms.

The Clash

With themes ranging from the queen of England to the hookers of Soho, from the streets of London to the highrise blocks of suburbia, for the first time since the heyday of the mods a decade and more before, English groups wanted to address English concerns and The Clash was at the top of the class. *I'm So Bored With The USA* notwithstanding, two of the combo's most crucial early songs, *London's Burning* and *Janie Jones* (about a high class madame whose activities had so recently been titillating the UK tabloids — and who would one day record a single of her own with The Clash) were all but indecipherable to non-Anglo ears and not only because Strummer had a voice like a lovesick water buffalo. *1977* warned of "stenguns in Knightsbridge"; *Deny* mentioned the 100 Club; even *Protex Blue*, titularly an ode to the US brand contraceptive, threw in a mention of the Bakerloo subway Line.

On July 4, The Clash played their first ever live show opening for The Sex Pistols at the Black Swan pub in Sheffield. They'd been rehearsing for just a month at the time and the letters' page in the Sounds music paper the following week gave a scathing report on their progress so far. "An anonymous music lover" reported, "Clash were just a cacophonous barrage of noise."

Over the next three months, through the first awakening of the punk scene, The Clash played regularly, undeterred by such criticism. The Sex Pistols, of course, were already established as the market leaders, but all around them, other rascals were breaking through — The Stranglers, old and crusty though they were, nevertheless had an attitude and a brutality which fit the prevalent times like a glove. Jones' old London SS mucker Brian James had The Damned up-and-running. The SS's third member, Tony James, was already rehearsing with what would soon become Chelsea.

From the start, though, The Clash seemed more real than any of them. Harder and harsher than they ever appeared on vinyl, stronger than they sounded in subsequent live shows, on a good night the 1976 vintage Clash could indeed match The Sex Pistols in almost every department, musically, lyrically and, increasingly, visually. Shopping at Oxfam, then converting even the dullest threads into Jackson Pollock-esque spatters, The Clash took a look in which Sex Pistol Glen Matlock had already been photographed, and made it their own. Matlock, after all, looked like someone who'd been messy while decorating. The Clash, on the other hand, looked absolutely marvelous — and they celebrated by writing a song in the spirit of the Modern Lovers' *Pablo Picasso*: "I don't give a bollock about Jackson Pollock." Sadly they never completed it.

On August 13, 1976, Rhodes unveiled his proteges to the London media with a showcase at their Ladbroke Grove rehearsal room. Two weeks later, they joined the newly formed Buzzcocks to open for the Pistols at the Islington Screen On The Green. A second show with the Pistols followed at the 100 Club on August 31. But just five days later, Keith Levine played his final gig as a member of the group, as they opened for pub rock heroes the Kursaal Flyers at the Roundhouse.

It was a gruelling show, made all the worse by the (mostly seated) audience's refusal to pay the band any attention whatsoever. Levine apparently agreed with them. He quit and later, explained why — "I wasn't into politics." And right now, that was all that The Clash was into.

The group opted not to replace Levine, debuting as a quartet at the 100 Club Punk Festival on September 20 — and furthering their stance when they refused to allow another of the scheduled bands, Siouxsie and the Banshees, to borrow their equipment because Siouxsie was wearing a swastika armband. At a time when the ultra-right wing National Front party was threatening to become a serious force in British politics (at a time, too, when the Rock Against Racism organization was just making its first inroads into the collective consciousness), The Clash's alarm was understandable. However, it also sparked an inter-punk rivalry which matched the Beatles vs. Stones debate in terms of manic intensity.

The Banshees bore The Clash no ill-will — they just borrowed the Pistols gear and got on with their show. Malcolm McLaren, however, was delighted. He, too, had flirted with swastika imagery around his Kings Road boutique, Sex — not out of any sense of solidarity with fascism, but because he enjoyed the shocked and horrified response which its gratuitous employment engendered.

The Clash's reaction confirmed what McLaren had already suspected for some time: that beneath their rebellious facade, The Clash was no different from any other group out there — they just wanted to be Rock and Roll stars. He already knew that The Clash represented the only threat to the Pistols' position at the peak of the punk pile. He now knew he was going to have to keep an even closer eye on their progress — and undermine it at every opportunity he got, ensuring that whatever else befell the band, their star would remain firmly affixed to the Pistols' own bandwagon.

Things were moving quickly for The Clash. A string of low-key headline gigs in and around London had already brought them a degree of press attention, particularly after they put together a well received show at the London ICA on October 23 under the banner A Night Of Pure Energy.

Polydor was loudly interested in The Clash and, in November, the label financed a two day demo session for the group, pairing them with former Mott the Hoople producer Guy Stevens. The sessions went well and Polydor's interest increased. Everything was moving ahead — it was time for McLaren to swoop. He invited The Clash to join The Sex Pistols' forthcoming nationwide ANARCHY tour, well aware that were they to refuse, they would shatter every last thread of unity within the very punk "scene" they were battling to create, but also well aware how much their position on the bill would rankle. They were, of course, at the bottom, behind The Damned and The Heartbreakers.

If The Clash was at all aggrieved, they never showed it. The chances are, however, that they didn't even notice — they already had enough on their plates as it was, as Terry Chimes quit just two weeks before the first show.

He was replaced by one Rob Harper, in which form The Clash joined a tour that started out with such high hopes, only to rapidly degenerate into a series of pointless bus rides, interspersed with the news that another local council had refused permission for The Sex Pistols and their chums to play in their town.

The Clash remained unbowed. Polydor was still chasing them, and on January 1, 1977, the band headlined the official opening night of the new punk venue, the Roxy. And though they never played there again, still they turned up to hang out with DJ Don Letts, purveyor of the coolest reggae sound system in town. Like virtually every other fashion in the genre, punk's almost symbiotic relationship with reggae was spawned at the Roxy — and once again, The Clash was in on the ground floor, so when it came time to fuse the two together, The Clash grabbed the golden ring by recording Junior Murvin's *Police And Thieves*.

"Now I think what a bold brass neck we had to cover it," Strummer marvelled years later. "But I'm glad we did, because . . . it led onto great things in the future with Lee Perry and Bob Marley hearing it, and being hip enough to know we'd brought our own music to the party."

Having flirted with Polydor for close to three months, The Clash finally signed with rival major CBS in late January, for an unheard-of 100,000 pounds — unheard of, that is, for a group that had been together just seven months, played no more than three dozen shows, and didn't even have a permanent drummer. Rob Harper had quit, and while Terry Chimes was willing to help out as much as he could, he was adamant that there would be no permanent reunion. Still, it was he who played on the combo's first single, *White Riot*, and he who would do the honors on *Police And Thieves*.

The Clash's version of *Police And Thieves* was built around a dramatic Mick Jones rearrangement, with two guitars playing the on and off-beats. It was, as Strummer later pointed out, an utterly unique styling — "any other group would've played on the offbeat [alone]." Indeed, when the song was first brought up, Strummer's own initial reaction was "'great, a reggae tune, let's do it like Hawkwind.' But Mick was more intelligent."

Playing through the song in the studio, learning to relax within the rhythm, The Clash reinvented *Police And Thieves* for Rock and Roll without even beginning to ruffle its own musical equilibrium, imbibing the performance with a roughness which assimilated the rebel soul of reggae at the same time as confirming the raging heart of punk. The result was a true hybrid, a garage skank attack which not only stands head and shoulders above the rest of the material being lined up for The Clash's debut album, it dwarfed almost anything being done in the name of punk at that time.

Neither were the six minutes given over to the song to be The Clash's only nod towards reggae. If that had been the case, the entire performance might well have ended up reeking of tokenism or worse. Johnny Rotten, after all, had only recently hissed that white groups trying to play reggae was a form of cultural exploitation.

Throughout their repertoire, the band — Jones in particular — experimented with sounds and ideas they'd picked up from the Jamaican records which Simonon and Strummer were stockpiling: drop-outs, phasing, so many little snatches which may not even have been noticeable individually, but together, conjured up the picture of a very English record, cut through with very Kingston stylings.

The album complete, The Clash returned to the road in March, 1977, still without a permanent drummer. Future Culture Clubber Jon Moss was set to join, but bailed shortly before his first gig, preferring to form his own group, London, instead. Again, Terry Chimes stepped in for a show at the Harlesden Colosseum. Hopefully, he wore a T-shirt emblazoned with the word "Goodbye," but of course it wasn't. The following month he was back in the studio with The Clash, cutting two tracks, *Capital Radio* and the instrumental *Listen*, for a single being released as a mail order incentive to New Musical Express readers.

Capital Radio was the latest blow in The Clash's on-going war with British broadcasting. *White Riot* had faltered at a lowly No. 38, with very little radio support to help push it higher. Now The Clash was out for revenge. They had already worked up a version of the Modern Lovers' *Roadrunner*, replacing the familiar refrain of "radio on" with a sneering "Radio One," aimed at the BBC's flagship rock and pop station. Even more radically, they blew out a prestigious session for the same station's JOHN PEEL SHOW. According to Peel himself, "[they] did the backing tracks, but couldn't do the vocals — they said the equipment wasn't up to the expected standards, which I thought wasn't a terribly revolutionary gesture."

Now it was independent radio's turn to be taunted. Despite broadcasting exclusively to the London area, Capital had remained singularly unsupportive of punk rock (programming director Aidan Day was singled out by name in the song), and had already been attacked once by The Clash, when they descended upon the station's offices one morning and spraypainted WHITE RIOT across the building's plate-glass frontage.

The station owners remained unmoved by both the paint and the record. A new Clash single, the album's *Remote Control* (backed by a blistering live version of *London's Burning*) fared even more poorly than its predecessor and so The Clash did the only thing they could do. They turned their wrath upon their record company, for releasing *Remote Control* in the first place.

They were furious, they said. They were never even consulted about this second single and they would never have sanctioned it if they had been — their choice, already announced in Melody Maker, was *Janie Jones*. The label had ridden roughshod over those demands, not out of any sense of commercial purpose, but because (or so it seemed), they could, to remind these uppity young punks just who was really in control.

Of course The Clash would get their own back. With the hapless Chimes having finally been allowed home, and yet another London SS veteran, Nicky "Topper" Headon installed, The Clash linked with reggae legend Lee "Scratch" Perry and returned to the studio to cut a new song, Jones' *Complete Control*, for release as their next 45. And while cynics wondered whether all parties concerned really were telling the truth — a record company which so abuses a band's trust is hardly likely to immediately follow through with a single telling the world of their own perfidy — *Complete Control* promptly gave the group their first Top 30 hit, reaching No. 28.

That their liaison with Lee Perry contrarily produced a decidedly rock-oriented song only increases the admiration with which one must regard this particular sequence. Perry's original mix was indeed rooted in reggae and dub techniques, and many other bands would have stuck with that whatever the end result sounded like. The Clash, however, realized when something just didn't feel right and, the moment Perry was gone, Mick Jones remixed the song completely, subverting the rhythm, raising the guitars, completely restructuring the piece. Even more radically, a version of the Maytals' *Pressure Drop*" (a live favorite through The Clash's spring 1977 White Riot tour) recorded at the same session was scrapped altogether.

"Lee Perry was brilliant," engineer Mickey Foote recalled. "He's a wild guy and he was shit hot. He took this equalizer and twiddled this bass dial around to the deep bass and the whole studio was shaking! He nearly blew the studio up trying to get Paul a bass sound." But Jones continued, "we went back and fiddled about . . . a bit. It was good what he did, but it sounded underwater slightly, his echo sound on us." (The group would subsequently rerecord *Pressure Drop* for the B-side of *English Civil War*, a song based around the forces favorite *When Johnny Comes Marching Home Again*, and again the juxtaposition was startling, rocked up reggae and reggae-flavored folk side by side on one crucial platter.)

Clash City Rockers was next, the first of several earnest attempts by the band to mythologize themselves á la Mott The Hoople's occasional autobiographical stabs, and an inspired effort which simultaneously ushered in what amounted to The Clash's own golden age of Rock and Roll.

If The Clash was hell-bent on forging their own sacrosanct place in the annals of Rock and Roll, however, they also remained acutely aware of all that was going on around them. In later years, it became very fashionable to condemn The Clash for never following through on the original promise and intentions of punk rock, as though they alone were to blame for the movement's eventual slide into onanistic incontinence. Yet as early as spring 1978, Strummer was well aware that this particular revolution was never going to happen — and said so in song, in the most important of all The Clash's early 45's, *(White Man) In Hammersmith Palais.*

Musically the song is peerless, following through the threat of *Police And Thieves* with a tight rocker rhythm spat out through seething guitars. But it was lyrically that *(White Man)* came into its own. In essence, it was based on Strummer's experiences at a Dillinger show at the west London venue, watching as an apparently unified black and white audience nevertheless divided down stereotypical cultural lines, "black sticksmen . . . running around trying to snatch these white girls' handbags," as Strummer later explained.

Yet from pondering the social divisions which that scenario raised, the song then narrowed its focus even further, to discuss the equally real schisms which were already tearing punk apart, and the continued ascent of groups who were so desperate to distance themselves from the now passé "fashion" of punk that they were now forgetting the meaning of it as well. Groups clad in "Burton suits . . . changing their votes . . . turning rebellion into money" . . . groups like the Jam, whose distinctly Burton suited vocalist, Paul Weller, had recently told the New Musical Express that despite the working class roots his music unhesitatingly drew from, he personally would be voting for the Conservative right at the next election.

Later, of course, the daft lad would confess that he'd simply been confused at the time, that he would never have voted for anything so hateful as Margaret Thatcher's blue-rinse repressors. At the time, however, Weller's words appeared as heartfelt as any of his other lofty pontifications and Strummer's lyric reflected a lot of people's rage, dismay — and confusion. If punk couldn't trust its own leaders, who could it trust?

The answer, of course, was nobody, because everybody lets you down in the end. First and foremost, punk was a creed of individualism, an umbrella under which a host of disparate beliefs and opinions could gather, not because they agreed with one another's ends, but because they didn't disagree. The Tom Robinson Band comprehended this, espousing vocalist Robinson's militant gay rhetoric, but supporting causes which ranged from womens' rights to anti-racism. The Adverts understood it, obliquely condemning the mentality of the masses in *Safety In Numbers* and then openly warning (in *I Surrender*) that "birds of a feather drop dead together — and that's all."

The Clash, however, still adhered to the vague notion that the collective "we" — the punks — were all in it together, that if the kids remained united, they could never be divided. If The Clash did then ultimately betray the revolution, it was because they so fervently believed there was a revolution to betray in the first place. There wasn't — there was just an unending sequence of isolated uprisings.

It's ironic, then, that both *Tommy Gun* (backed by a studio version of *1,2 Crush On You*) and *English Civil War* — their next two singles — should acknowledge that fact, even as

The Clash themselves continued to argue for some semblance of "togetherness." Ironic, too, that both singles should fall within the immediate vicinity of what was to prove The Clash's foulest musical error yet, the album GIVE 'EM ENOUGH ROPE.

According to legend, it was the US wing of the band's label that first suggested they try working with producer Sandy Pearlman, best known for the bludgeoning epics he'd wrung out of the Blue Oyster Cult. The Clash themselves denied this, insisting that it was their idea to bring him in — although whether that was any better is debatable. Either way, the target was the same, to follow through on the 100,000+ sales that imports of their debut had racked up in the US, and give The Clash an album which could impact upon American radio without detracting from their inherent visceral attack.

They succeeded, too. GIVE 'EM ENOUGH ROPE emerged slick and shining, drenched in big rock guitars and drums, and littered with the self-conscious self-mythology which — by comparison — the band had only flirted with in the past. *All The Young Punks (New Boots And Contracts)* offered up a history of the Clash-so-far, painting our heroes as loveable, defiant, yet sorely misunderstood ruffians who only wanted what was best for the kids. *Last Gang In Town* dramatized of the group's role as self-appointed vigilantes of Rock and Roll. *Cheapskates* bemoaned the number of people who found the whole stance just a little overdone. A number, of course, which would increase a thousandfold once they heard the album.

The band had split with manager Rhodes by now, installing first journalist Caroline Coon, and then former Pink Floyd managers Blackhill Enterprises in his place. Rhodes' plans for The Clash remained largely unaffected, however, including the wizard notion of having them star in their very own movie, a "wayward youth makes good" type study of the power of Rock and Roll. Of course it didn't work out that way — RUDIE CAN'T FAIL, the project's original, self-affirming title, was ultimately shortened to RUDE BOY alone, as Rudie not only failed, he bollocks-ed up big time. The Clash's dreams were further shattered when they discovered they didn't even own rights in the movie — Rhodes had sold them off before he departed.

Only the live footage saved the day. Shot throughout the group's late 1977 / early 1978 UK tours, culminating with their impassioned performance at an Anti-Nazi League carnival in east London in April 1978, RUDE BOY offered up some genuinely dramatic music, incontrovertible evidence that no matter how wretched their recent performances on vinyl and in print might be (no-one could give crasser interviews than The Clash!), in concert they still had no peers.

In early 1979, The Clash returned to the studio with first album producer Bill Price to cut a return to form, a return to basics, the COST OF LIVING EP. It comprised four tracks — a cover of *I Fought The Law*, a new version of *Capital Radio*, a rerecorded ROPE outtake called *Groovy Times* and the prehistoric reject *Ooh Baby Ooh*, rewritten as *Gates Of The West* and partially recorded in New York in September 1978, while Strummer and Jones were on a brief promotional visit.

Four old songs, then, restating an old direction, but the EP was so much more than that. It was the formulation of a new era for the band, restating the sense of wide eyed musical adventure which had characterized their first strivings — and would now dictate their future. The Clash had tried to follow their record company's whims and ended up with egg on their faces (and ropes round their necks.) From here on in, they would do things their way.

The first statement of their newfound defiance came when they announced an eight date US tour in February 1979, despite Epic's insistence that they were wasting their time — GIVE 'EM ENOUGH ROPE had long since stopped selling, after all. They toured regardless, hiring Bo Diddley as support (another source of label dismay), and wound up selling out all eight shows. That, too, proved to the group that their own instincts were the only ones they could rely upon, but even devoted fans were to be shocked by just how seriously The Clash would now take that dictate.

Anxious to capitalize on this sudden reversal, Epic rush-released a domestic US edition of the band's debut album, manhandled into more contemporary shape by the substitution of sundry recent singles for four of the original set's more parochial cuts (complete control again!) The Clash, meanwhile, returned to the studio to concoct LONDON CALLING, the set which would finally establish them as a genuine force in the land.

Reuniting with Guy Stevens, producer of their first Polydor demos, the group warmed up by recording close to a dozen oldies, including an impassioned version of Vince Taylor's *Brand New Cadillac* — Taylor, of course, was another of rock's ragged cult heroes, a delinquent touchstone for any number of left field fantasies.

It is, of course, a great song, one of the archetypes for the girls and cars epics that remain the bedrock for so much classic Rock and Rroll. But The Clash did more than simply cover the song, they incorporated its spirit as well, subpoenaing Taylor's very reputation, applying it to producer Stevens' own maverick mythology and absorbing both into their own legend. And it worked. No longer the somewhat silly suburban revolutionaries who kept the music press in chuckles throughout 1978, The Clash was suddenly imbibed with a genuine street-smart glamor and chic, a guerilla force who daringly diced with the furthest extremes of creativity.

Stevens himself essentially left the sessions after but two weeks of recording, during which he demonstrated that every past rumor of his eccentricity was true. He retained his production credit, though, and The Clash themselves would not hear a word against him. When the producer died from a prescription drug overdose on August 29, 1981, they promptly recorded a tribute song, *Midnight To Stevens*. They would also credit him with "inspiration" for their COMBAT ROCK album — a backhanded compliment, given the nature of that particular disc, but a heartfelt one regardless. Maybe Stevens didn't contribute much to the physical recording of LONDON CALLING, but his spirit was all over it.

Rockabilly, bluesy jazz, pop, R&B, reggae, lover's rock, The Clash assaulted them all. But LONDON CALLING was no dilettante exercise in jack-of-all-tradesmanship. Each song was performed with almost startling finesse and feeling, while the lyrical themes were equally all encompassing. The famous and the forgotten, pushers and losers, the disillusioned and the lost, hoods, heroes and cheats all took their places across the six week sessions. And if the strongest songs were the most radical — the title track, *Working For The Clampdown, Guns Of Brixton* — by moving beyond the constraints of even the most indulgent onlookers' expectations, still the overall vision was a triumph.

While the ever-faithful Bill Price mixed the album during September 1979, The Clash toured the US for the second time that year (the Clash Take The Fifth tour), then, returning home from a fractious, but ultimately wildly successful outing, they went back into the studio to record what would become their ultimate contribution to the garage skank fusion, a bass blurged apocalypso version of Willie Weeks' classic *Armagideon Time*.

Armagideon Time was originally brought into the group's repertoire as a soundcheck warm-up, then promoted to an incendiary encore. In both instances, The Clash stripped it back to its bass-driven basics, from which they developed a driving jam, Strummer growling the lyric over one of Simonon, Jones' and Headon's most unified performances yet. Even more powerfully, they then extended the original song into genuine dub territory, emerging with a ten minute epic which would as thoroughly redirect rock reggae as *Police And Thieves* had reinvented it two years previous. Indeed, in the annals of punk-and-after's manifold experiments with such a fusion, only The Ruts' *Jah Wars* even came close to equalling The Clash's accomplishment. Everyone else was left at the starting gate.

But would there be room for such an epic on the album? Even excluding the three days worth of covers recorded with Stevens at the start of the sessions, the group had some 20 tracks ready for release, far too many to fit onto a single album, but almost all of them more or less an essential element in the overall picture.

It was their American label which came to the rescue — albeit utterly unknowingly. The US version of THE CLASH arrived with a free single, presenting two tracks (*Groovy Times* and *Gates Of The West*) which hadn't fit onto the album itself. When The Clash suggested they make a similar gesture with their new album, CBS readily agreed. Perhaps, the band then continued, it could be a 12-inch single? Again, CBS could see no problem. Only when the group announced that instead of having two or three tracks revolving at 45 rpm, the single would have eight or nine spinning at 33 did the label realize precisely what they had committed themselves to, by which time it was too late. The Clash had pulled off a marketing coup-de-grace, a double album which retailed for the price of a single set. ("*Armagideon Time* didn't make the album, turning up instead on the B-side of the band's next single, *London Calling*.)

LONDON CALLING was released in December 1979 and left the critics perplexed. In Britain, the growing Americanization of the group's vision remained a thorny subject — even its deliciously homesick title track took on extra significance following the recent near-meltdown of the Three Mile Island nuclear power plant. But The Clash had irrefutably retained their own vision (the inclusion of five further ska / reggae numbers alone proved that.) While pedantic onlookers delved deep inside the lyrics to isolate further Yankophiliac tendencies, LONDON CALLING remained a defiantly English album, as Strummer acknowledged three years later. "I never thought about beefburgers once," he pledged.

The six months preceding the release of LONDON CALLING had seen the UK scene undergo another of its periodic seismic changes, this time in the form of both the 2-Tone ska resurgence and a collaborative Mod revival. Neither meant much in America, but both ricochetted throughout LONDON CALLING, and with good reason.

The Specials, titular heads of the ska movement (and willing protagonists in the mod), had themselves landed their first major break opening for The Clash the previous year. Unashamedly, they drew their musical inspiration from many of the same sources (and scratchy old Trojan label albums.) And unapologetically, they threw themselves towards notions which The Clash had hitherto owned exclusive rights to, writing new rock songs around old ska rhythms, updating classics and making them their own and, most of all, painting a picture of a society which had firmly embraced its own self-destruction — 1979 also saw Margaret Thatcher come to power.

Now, while she invoked the specters of the draft and restricted immigration as short sharp cures for the evils of unemployment, The Specials joined The Clash as the loudest (commercially viable) voices raised against her. The 2-Tone group had already published their manifesto in the form of a devastating debut album. The Clash, recognizing much of their own blueprint in those same grooves, were now duty bound to respond in kind. And LONDON CALLING was only

the first volley. The next twelve months of The Clash's career were to be devoted to a spree of musical insurrection unparalleled since the heady days of psychedelia.

Two successive singles, the deep dub *Bankrobber* and the brittle skank *The Call Up*, kept the band buoyant through much of 1981. A UK tour with reggae vocalist Mikey Dread (who also produced *Bankrobber*) saw The Clash simply sparking with live wire energy. And a return to the US saw Rolling Stone, of all graying institutions, welcome them with one of the most honest appraisals they'd received in three years, a front cover headlined "Rebels with a cause and a hit album."

Even the loss of Paul Simonon for six weeks, as he shot scenes for the movie LADIES AND GENTLEMEN, THE FABULOUS STAINS (the story of an all girl rock group), could not dampen the band's creativity. Ensconced in New York City's Iroquois Hotel, Jones, Strummer and Headon simply borrowed Norman Watt Roy from Ian Dury's Blockheads and got on with recording.

The Clash

Some masterful material emerged from those sessions — covers of the Equals' *Police On My Back* and Spencer Davis' *Every Little Bit Hurts*; a tribute to the Sugarhill Gang, *The Magnificent Seven*; a funky dub monster called *Lightning Strikes (Not Once But Twice)* . . . much of this material would remain in the can for the next decade, until being exhumed for the CLASH ON BROADWAY boxed-set. But if history regards these songs as mere out-takes or the fruit of an unused studio session, history (as so often) has its head in the sand. The Clash's next album, the triple disc set SANDANISTA, would be roundly condemned as being two discs too long. But the best of it, coupled with the unused portions of the New York sessions, could have created a double album to rival LONDON CALLING. And adding the US-only BLACK MARKET CLASH compilation to the brew would have assured its immortality.

Despite a title (and a series of period interviews) which certainly pointed towards a lofty concept of some sort, SANDANISTA was nothing more than a snapshot of three weeks in the life of The Clash, rolling the tapes and playing whatever came into their heads. Intending initially simply to complete material worked up in New York, at the legendary Channel One studios in Jamaica and at Manchester's Pluto Studios (where *Bankrobber* took shape), the band retired to Wessex Studios and began work. However, they also continued writing, ending up with 30+ tracks which they worked on with near-obsessive zeal, the already marathon 12-13 hour sessions sometimes stretching around the clock, if the mood was right.

Again the group delved into every stylistic box they could squeeze their nerve into. Again, the results were as sprawling as they were impressive and, this time, accusations of rampant self-indulgence were not far from the truth. There really was no need for The Clash to have recorded so many songs and there was certainly no need for them to release them all.

The UK media, whose feelings towards The Clash had again swung into the negative regions, hammered SANDANISTA with pitbull passion, and the band's inability (or unwillingness) to explain their true motives only sharpened the axes. Still obsessed by The Clash's apparent adoption of and by the US, British journalists peered under every stone on the record in search of the telltale stars and stripes.

Even when faced by a virtual album's worth of reggae and dub, music which the US had thus far proven inexplicably resilient to, some of Britain's finest journalistic minds accused the group of selling their soul to the land of the highest bidder, a patriotic misogyny which reached unparalleled peaks of silliness when New Musical Express journalist Nick Kent slammed Strummer for not singing enough songs about the hell of Thatcher's Britain — as though simply living in it wasn't bad enough for the average teenaged listener.

The Clash took the criticism on the chin. They recorded an album with Jones' girlfriend, Ellen Foley, turning in a reflective set which had far more in common with Edith Piaf than political comment. They cut two new singles, *This Is Radio Clash* and *Know Your Rights*. And they reunited with former manager Bernie Rhodes, admitting that though they might not always agree with his methods, at least he knew what the band was about. Traveling on through a year beset by personal problems, not least of all drummer Headon's increasingly disruptive relationship with heroin, they toured Britain, Europe and the US, an outing which climaxed with an unprecedented and now, utterly legendary 16 show residency at Bonds in New York City.

They recorded another single with New York graffiti artist Futura 2000 (*The Escapades Of Futura 2000*) and yet another with Janie Jones, of first album song fame, under the suitably abbreviated name of the Lash. They worked with beat poet Allen Ginsberg. Jones alone produced Theatre Of Hate's breakthrough WESTWORLD album. And at the end of it all, they cut COMBAT ROCK, the most successful album in the group's entire catalog — and one of the worst records made by any graduate of Britain's school of punk rock heroes.

The album sessions themselves were as productive and inspired as any the band had ever held. Determined to bang it out as quickly as possible and to keep it short for the first time since ROPE, The Clash drew upon all the experiences of the previous year — not least of all the excitement they had felt in New York, turning on the radio to listen to rap and dance music, and encountering the DJs' private remixes of their own *Magnificent Seven*. Graffiti and ghetto blasters were the new weapons with which the revolution would be fought, and The Clash could not wait to slam their impressions down.

In their haste to start work, however, they forgot to pack the one thing which they had always been able to rely upon — their own unique sense of unity. Though Headon had returned from Planet Smack to write the music for the memorable *Rock The Casbah* (he would play drums, piano and bass on the final cut), Jones appeared more interested in behaving like a rock star than working as one. The seeds of his eventual dismissal from The Clash were as apparent in his contributions to COMBAT ROCK as in the roots of his next project, Big Audio Dynamite, and already existed in the manic throb of the Theatre Of Hate album he'd been working on. Jones' big number on COMBAT ROCK would also prove to be one of two extraordinarily prophetic titles on the set, *Should I Stay Or Should I Go?*. The other was *Straight To Hell*.

Grimly adhering to the album's working title, RAT PATROL FROM FORT BRAGG, much of COMBAT ROCK dealt with Strummer's vision of inner city America as an urban Vietnam. But the songs were less than sketches, the tunes were less than musical and veteran producer Glyn Johns' listless AOR-inspired final mix was even more out of place than Sandy Pearlman's big rock guitar approach.

Indeed, once past the *Casbah* and *Should I Stay* hit singles that propelled the album to the stars, *Straight To Hell* (which itself encapsulated many of Strummer's new pet themes) was the only genuinely great Clash song on the record. The fact that it was also one of the greatest Clash songs ever perhaps adds further piquancy to its brooding intensity. That one song captured everything that The Clash should have been capable of in 1982-83. The remainder of COMBAT ROCK, meanwhile, had just one thing in its favor — Jones' request that they make it a 15 track double album was shot down by his bandmates.

Clearly at odds both with one another and the world in general, The Clash struggled on, even as their record sales went through the roof. Headon quit for a solo career in May 1982. He was replaced, perhaps inevitably, by original drummer Terry Chimes and in this form, the group toured the US both in their own right and opening for the Who through September. Chimes then departed again, and when The Clash returned to the US in May, 1983, it was with the previously unknown Pete Howard on drums. Weeks later, Mick Jones was sacked.

The Clash's final show was their largest ever, appearing in front of 140,000 people at Glen Helen regional park in Los Angeles. They received half a million dollars for performing, came onstage two hours late, and played an 80 minute set before departing. It was both a highly fitting and a desperately ignominious end to the group's career.

Jones' departure was not made public until September 1983, by which time his own next project, Big Audio Dynamite, was already underway. Strummer, Howard and Simonon, meantime, recruited two new musicians, Nick Sheppard and Vince White, and gamely soldiered on, touring Europe and the US through 1984, and even releasing a new album, 1985's CUT THE CRAP. But with the music press splitting its sides at the sight of them and the record buying public having found other records to buy, the outfit was doomed from the outset. The Clash broke up, barely noticed and scarcely mourned, in January 1986.

Strummer and Jones promptly reunited over the course of Big Audio Dynamite's second album, and there were widespread rumors that they might reform The Clash. Of course they didn't — Strummer, too, had a solo career in mind. But the rumor mill kept grinding nevertheless.

The appearance of the STORY OF THE CLASH VOLUME ONE compilation in 1988 immediately prompted speculation that the original line-up would regroup to commence VOLUME TWO. The announcement of 1994's CLASH ON BROADWAY boxed-set raised hopes that Strummer, Jones and Simonon would at least tape a few new songs to round the package out. Neither scenario came to pass.

When *Should I Stay Or Should I Go?* topped the UK chart following its adoption for as Levis commercial in 1991, even the group's closest former associates could not believe that The Clash were not reforming to capitalise upon their good fortune, while this year's reactivation of the band's entire catalog (CUT THE CRAP excluded), together with the live album FROM HERE TO ETERNITY, offered them yet another chance to recreate that old Clash magic. But once again they turned it down, just as they've refused the checks the size of telephone numbers that have periodically been brandished at them; just as they have doggedly remained true to the original decision to split, even as almost every one of their erstwhile contemporaries have regrouped for one more go round the town. Maybe they really did mean everything they said back then.

CLASH DISCOGRAPHY
UK Singles
  ○ *White Riot / 1977* (CBS 5058, 1977)
  ○ *Capital Radio / Listen /* interview (NME / CBS CL1, 1977)
  ○ *Remote Control / London's Burning* (CBS 5293, 1977)
  ○ *Complete Control / City Of The Dead* (CBS 5664, 1977)

- Clash City Rockers / Jail Guitar Doors (CBS 5834, 1978)
- (White Man) In Hammersmith Palais / Prisoner (CBS 6383, 1978)
- Tommy Gun / 1, 2, Crush On You (CBS 6788, 1978)
- English Civil War / Pressure Drop (CBS 7082, 1979)
- COST OF LIVING EP (CBS 7324, 1979)
- London Calling / Armagideon Time (CBS 8087, 1979)
- London Calling / Armagideon Time / Justice Tonight / Kick It Over (12")
  (CBS 128087, 1979)
- Bank Robber / Rockers Galore (CBS 8323, 1980)
- The Call Up / Stop The World (CBS 9339, 1980)
- Hitsville UK / Radio One (CBS 9480, 1981)
- The Magnificent Seven / The Magnificent Dance (CBS A1133, 1981)
- This Is Radio Clash / Radio Clash (CBS 1797, 1981)
- This Is Radio Clash / Radio Clash / Radio Five / Outside Broadcast (12")
  (CBS A121797, 1981)
- Know Your Rights / First Night Back In London (CBS A2309, 1982)
- Rock the Casbah / Long Time Jerk (CBS A2479, 1982)
- Rock The Casbah / Long Time Jerk / Mustapha Dance (CBS A122479, 1982)
- Should I Stay Or Should I Go / Straight To Hell (CBS A2646, 1982)
- This Is England / Do It Now (CBS A6122, 1985)
- This Is England / Do It Now / Sex Mad Roar (12") (CBS A122646, 1985)

US Singles

- I Fought The Law / (White Man) In Hammersmith Palais (Epic 50738, 1979)
- Train In Vain / London Calling (Epic 50851, 1980)
- Hitsville UK / Police On My Back (Epic 51013, 1981)
- The Call Up / The Cool Out / Magnificent Dance (Epic 02036, 1981)
- Should I Stay Or Should I Go / Inoculated City (Epic 03006, 1982)
- Should I Stay Or Should I Go / First Night Back In London (Epic 03061, 1982)
- Rock The Casbah / Long Time Jerk (Epic 03245, 1982)
- Should I Stay Or Should I Go / Cool Confusion (Epic 03547, 1983)

UK Albums

- THE CLASH (CBS 82000, 1977)
- GIVE 'EM ENOUGH ROPE (CBS 82431, 1978)
- LONDON CALLING (CBS CLASH 3, 1979)
- SANDANISTA (CBS FSLN 1, 1980)
- CONCERTS FOR THE PEOPLE OF KAMPUCHEA (compilation including
  Armagideon Time, live) (Atlantic K60153, 1981)
- COMBAT ROCK (CBS FMLN 2, 1982)
- CUT THE CRAP (CBS 26601, 1985)
- THE STORY OF THE CLASH VOLUME ONE (compilation) (CBS 460244, 1988)
- THE SINGLES (compilation) (CBS 4689461, 1991)
- THE TWELVE INCH MIXES (CBS 450123, 1991)
- ON BROADWAY (boxed-set) (CBS 4284, 1992)
- SUPER BLACK MARKET CLASH (compilation) (Epic 474546, 1993)

US Albums

- ° GIVE 'EM ENOUGH ROPE (Epic 35543, 1978)
- ° THE CLASH (US version) (Epic 36060, 1979)
- ° LONDON CALLING (Epic 36328, 1980)
- ° SANDANISTA! (Epic 37037, 1980)
- ° COMBAT ROCK (Epic 37689, 1982)
- ° CUT THE CRAP (Epic 40017, 1985)
- ° BLACK MARKET CLASH (Epic 36846, 1980)
- ° THE STORY OF THE CLASH VOLUME ONE (Epic 44035, 1988)
- ° THE SINGLES (Epic 63886, 1991)
- ° SUPER BLACK MARKET CLASH (Epic 474546, 1993)
- ° ON BROADWAY (boxed-set) (Epic 46991, 1994)
- ° ROCKERS GALORE (Epic 47144, 1999)
- ° FROM HERE TO ETERNITY (Epic 65747, 1999)

⋖ 3 ⋗
The Damned

No-one would have predicted it, but the Damned are THE great survivors of punk. First to release a single, first to visit America, first to cut an album, they were also the first to break up. But two decades on, The Damned — or at least, "a" Damned — are still going strong, seldom appearing with less than two original members on board, and occasionally threatening to hit the old heights as well. Even today, you write them off at your own risk.

The Damned came together in 1976 when Brian James, fresh from the still-born hopefulness of the London SS, encountered drummer Chris "Rat Scabies" Miller, himself passing through an SS audition in between rehearsals for the PUSS IN BOOTS pantomime he was drumming in.

Johnny Moped guitarist Ray "Captain Sensible" Burns was next in, and as a trio, the band — dubbed the Subterraneans for the occasion — made its live debut in Cardiff, Wales, backing NME journalist and hopeful would-be rock god Nick Kent at a couple of shows. Back in London, though, they discovered a singer of their own — Dave "Vanian" Letts, a gravedigger with a penchant for dressing as Dracula and, by summer 1976, the newly named Damned were playing their own first show at what Scabies remembered as "some queer place in Lisson Grove."

From there, they graduated to the 100 Club, supporting The Sex Pistols. In August, they provided one of the best sets at the first Mont De Marsen punk festival in France. And the following month, The Damned catapulted punk rock into the tabloid headlines when a bottle, thrown at the stage during The Damned's set, shattered against a pillar. A girl standing nearby was hit in the face by glass. She ended up losing the sight in one eye.

Scabies recalled, "it's kind of a can of worms story now in some ways, because it was Sid [Vicious] that threw the glass, my publisher watched him do it. It was only later on that it all came to light, I didn't realize until five years later that he'd been arrested for it. It kind of sucked . . . there's nothing worse than being a sitting target, which you are on stage. What happens is, a couple of incidents will occur, and then it gets all over the papers, 'Violence, Violence, Violence,' and then suddenly everyone says, 'Waaahhh!'"

The group visited the girl in hospital and also tried to organize a benefit show. They could not find a suitable venue willing to book them — ironically, the fear of further violence was too great.

The drummer continues, "there was a lot of violence, but it was never from the Punks, never from us, but the local thuggery hanging about outside or the local football squad. You have to remember the cops and everybody turned their backs on everything. We [The Damned] did shows where cops would just drive away as 500 people trashed your van. But it wasn't the Punks that were doing it, it was more gang warfare. If you weren't a Punk, you went and hit one. And that became if you were a Punk, and you saw someone that wasn't, then they'd better look out, because if they gave you any shit, you'd hit them. That was pretty much from the off."

Chiswick was the first label to sense The Damned's potential, but Stiff beat them to the punch and in October, *New Rose* became the band's first single — and the first "punk" single ever, at long last serving up a reference point for the manifold musical streams and imaginings being focussed into place by the movement's press coverage.

Very early on, The Damned themselves dismissed attempts to file them away with the rest of the punk pack — Scabies preferred "Dole Rock or Street Rock, cos that's where our roots are," while James admitted that he was constantly arguing with Mick Jones — "He's into changing the political system, I want people to enjoy themselves and forget politics."

But The Damned were custom built for such pigeonholing regardless. Fast, loud and anarchic, a Damned gig was a celebration of everything punk portended, sloppiness and ineptitude included. The sound of The Damned was the sound of thunderous chaos, shot through with the two minute masterpieces which James was simply flicking off his pen —

The Damned

New Rose, their first single; *Neat Neat Neat*, their second; *Fan Club* and *Feel The Pain* from their thrice-eponymous debut album.

A musical cross between the MC5 and Mott The Hoople, Mud and METALLIC KO, T Rex and the Stooges, the album was a stunning, stunned return to basics which threw every last pretense of experience and expertise to the wind. The group's detractors thought themselves smart when they described The Damned as primitive. They were way off the mark — The Damned's fans saw them as positively primeval and, when the Flamin' Groovies described the group as "the worst musicians we've ever played with," the gulf between what was really old and new yawned even larger. Prior to that, the Groovies — like a lot of other, early-mid 70's American cults — had stood a chance of catching hold of British punk loyalties. With just one ill-considered condemnation, they slammed that door shut forever.

Not that the Damned themselves were immune to the occasional faux pas. Recruited to The Sex Pistols' ill-fated December 1976 ANARCHY tour, The Damned were sacked for admitting that they'd be happy to play even if the headliners were banned (which, in the wake of the Bill Grundy fiasco, they usually were.) Like The Stranglers, punk persona non grata since a well-publicized squabble with the Pistols outside Dingwalls during the summer, The Damned had committed a treason of sorts, shattering the facade of punk solidarity by looking out for themselves instead of putting the movement to the fore.

Of course they were — they admitted it often enough. But with the odd, twisted logic that did so much to shape punk sensibilities, swearing "we're not punk" was an admission that you were, for what better way to establish one's punk credentials than to do something so patently designed to destroy them? The Jam's Paul Weller figured that out when he burned a copy of *Sniffin' Glue* on stage and claimed he was going to be voting Conservative at the next election — punk was, perhaps, the only creed in history where you had to step as far outside as possible, before you could be accepted as being inside.

The Damned's protests, then, were always destined to fall on deaf ears, which meant that when they themselves practiced what they'd been preaching all along, the cry of treachery could be heard the length and breadth of the country.

The Damned didn't care. DAMNED DAMNED DAMNED arrived bristling with a set of songs which all but defined the popular (as in non-London-club based) notion of what a good punk group should sound like, while the group's pioneering trip to America would prove infinitely influential upon that country's nascent scene, even if one of their Boston shows was highlighted by the band sitting on stage tossing pizza at each other and the audience. Homegrown (and New York-centric) acts like Television, Patti Smith, the Talking Heads and Richard Hell's Voidoids had long since grown accustomed to being called punks by the UK press — The Damned's arrival showed them that musically, culturally and socially, they weren't even in the same ballpark.

Back in London, The Damned celebrated their first anniversary with three sold out nights at the London Marquee in July. Weeks later, The Damned augmented their line-up with a second guitarist, Robert "Lu" Edmunds, better to realize the fast changing songs with which James was supplying them. But it was not a happy family. Despite again going down a storm at the second Mont de Marsen festival, Scabies had had enough. Less than a month later, he faked a suicide bid and loudly left the group.

The Damned's second album, MUSIC FOR PLEASURE, was released a few days later. Scorned by Scabies as an attempt to mimic the Rolling Stones' SATANIC MAJESTIES album, produced by Pink Floyd's Nick Mason after the group's initial demands for Syd Barrett were misheard at record company level, and featuring vintage jazzman Lol Coxhill on loudly blurting sax, MUSIC FOR PLEASURE had nothing to do with The Damned, nothing to do with 1977, and wound up with nothing to do whatsoever.

Two singles, *Problem Child* and *Don't Cry Wolf*, fared no better than the album, but The Damned truly hit the low water mark on their next UK tour. With former London (and future Culture Club) drummer Jon Moss replacing Scabies, and support from New York's iconoclastic Dead Boys, The Damned found themselves playing to near-empty houses — near-empty, that is, aside from the battery of critics waiting to tear the group to shreds.

In January 1978, The Damned's manager, Dave Robinson, called it quits, taking the group's record contract with him. "This is a record company, not a museum," sniffed a Stiff Records spokesman. A month later, The Damned themselves conceded defeat, regrouping eight weeks later to play a final farewell.

James split for his own trans-magical psychedelic act, Tanz Der Youth, and a career which would take him to the greater heights of the Lords Of The New Church, a stint with Iggy Pop and a clutch of astounding solo albums — he remains one of the most powerful guitarists Britain has ever produced. His chums, meanwhile, scattered towards solo careers (Sensible and Scabies) and the Doctors Of Madness (Vanian), before reuniting within nine months, for a fresh bite at the pop cherry. And 20 years later, they're still around. No-one would EVER have predicted that.

THE DAMNED DISCOGRAPHY
UK Singles 1976-77
- *New Rose / Help* (Stiff BUY 6, 1976)
- *Neat Neat Neat / Stab Yor Bak / Singalongascabies* (Stiff BUY 10, 1977)
- *Stretcher Case Baby / Sick Of Being Sick* (Stiff DAMNED 1, 1977)
- *Problem Child / You Take My Money* (Stiff BUY 18, 1977)
- *Don't Cry Wolf / One Way Love* (Stiff BUY 24, 1977)

- THE DAMNED FOUR PACK EP (compilation including BUY 191911924)
  (Stiff GRAB 2, 1981)
- *Sick Of Being Sick / Stretcher Case Baby / Help / New Rose / Problem Child*
  (Stiff BUY 238, 1986)
- THE PEEL SESSION EP (1977): *Sick Of Being Sick / Stretcher Case Baby / Fan Club / Feel The Pain* (Strange Fruit SFPS 002, 1987)
- THE PEEL SESSION EP (1976): *Stab Yor Bak / Neat Neat Neat / New Rose / So Messed Up / I Fall* (Strange Fruit SFPS 040, 1987)

UK Albums
- DAMNED DAMNED DAMNED (Stiff SEEZ 1, 1977)
- MUSIC FOR PLEASURE (Stiff SEEZ 5, 1977)
- NOT THE CAPTAIN'S BIRTHDAY PARTY (live 1977) (Demon VEXCD 7, 1986)
- SKIP OFF SCHOOL TO SEE THE DAMNED (Demon VEXCD 12, 1992)
- NEAT NEAT NEAT (boxed-set) (Demon FBOOK 14, 1997)

⋖ 4 ⋗
The Vibrators

The Vibrators formed in February 1976, around the quartet of vocalist Ian "Knox" Carnochan, bassist Pat Collier, guitarist John Ellis and drummer Eddie. After making their live debut the following month at the Hornsey College of Art as support for The Stranglers, early gigs saw them opening for the likes of The Stranglers and the Pistols. By October, they were a shoo-in for the 100 Club Punk Festival, both in their own right and as back-up group for guest veteran Chris Spedding.

Their inclusion was an odd one, nevertheless. Their set was comprised exclusively of cover versions — and not particularly hip ones at that. At a time when Iggy, the Velvets and the Dolls were de rigueur, the Vibrators exercised the Stones (*Jumping Jack Flash*), The Beatles (*I Saw Her Standing There*), Jerry Lee Lewis (*Great Balls Of Fire*) and Chubby Checker (*Let's Twist Again*), with the biggest roar of the evening reserved for Spedding's *Motorbikin'*. At least that song had been released within living (1975) memory.

It was Spedding who paved the way for The Vibrators' first record deal when he introduced the group to his then-record label, RAK, and took them into the studio to cut their debut single, *We Vibrate*. History records that it was only just edged out (by The Damned's *New Rose*) in the then frenetic race to release the first ever punk single. The Vibrators, however, would come first in another battle, the first of the new groups to record a session for BBC radio's John Peel.

Taped on October 12 and broadcast two weeks later, The Vibrators' maiden session offers little indication of the group's intentions. Of five songs, only *I'm Gonna Be Your Nazi Baby* could even vaguely be construed as controversial (although another cut,

Dance To The Music, would later earn some media flack after its title changed to *Whips And Furs.*) Elsewhere, through *Sweet Sweetheart, Jenny Jenny* and *We Vibrate,* The Vibrators sounded as though they'd just graduated from the Pub Rock academy — a far cry indeed from the hellacious racket which The Damned would be kicking up in those same surroundings some six weeks later.

In November, the Vibrators were announced as one of the attractions of The Sex Pistols' forthcoming tour, alongside The Ramones and The Talking Heads. They pulled out when the New Yorkers decided not to go ahead with the visit and, in the immediate wake of The Sex Pistols' TODAY show appearance, were probably glad that they did so. As the Pistols' tour dates crumbled, The Vibrators could still look forward to a solidly booked round of shows both at home and in Holland, Belgium and Germany. They spoke too soon. By December 8, the entire tour had been cancelled as even dedicated promoters of punk ran scared from enraged local citizens.

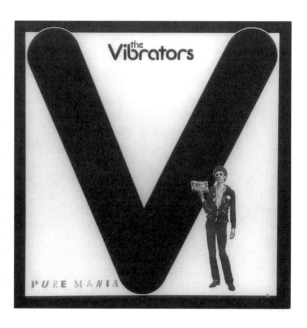

The Vibrators' second single, backing Spedding on his own tribute to the energies of punk, *Pogo Dancing,* was already out. Now there were plans for a third single, either a cover of *Jumping Jack Flash* or their own *Bad Time.* In any event, it was neither — the release was scrapped when the band quit RAK and, taking the opportunity to completely revamp their sound, re-emerged on Epic as an unrepentant barrage of pop-inflected adrenalin.

The band's Epic debut remains the archetypal Vibrators song — *Baby Baby* was built around a riff which, if it wasn't such bad form to say so, was cut straight from the classic rock mould, but delivered with an intensity that made a mockery of the song's moon-in-June-y lyrics. Certainly it established the group in the forefront of the punk movement, a standing which was only amplified first by their debut album, PURE MANIA, then when they landed the support slot on Iggy Pop's March 1977 UK comeback tour.

A second outing followed, with labelmate Ian Hunter, while the group's latest single, *London Girls,* was recorded live — further evidence of the band's now masterful approach to the stage. Only one black cloud hung over their heads, a vague suspicion that The Vibrators had almost painstakingly kept their name out of the less salubrious headlines to dog punk through spring 1977. They had never been arrested, never made the headlines, never spat at old ladies and Royalty. They just kept their heads down and worked their balls off.

In August, just as the group planned to move to Berlin, Pat Collier departed to form a new group, powerpop pioneers The Boyfriends. His decision rocked the band's equilibrium a little — although he wasn't their sole songwriter, he was largely responsible for the best of their canon, a skilful pop architect whose crafted licks would surely be missed. Yet his replacement, future Adam's Ant Gary Tibbs, arrived in time for The Vibrators' biggest hit ever, March 1978's *Automatic Lover*.

PURE MANIA, the group's second album, was built on the foundations laid by its predecessor. Again placing content over controversy, and again cut with an eye for a career in music as opposed to a mere 15 minutes of fame, the album sold well, but could do nothing to prevent the continued erosion of the group's personnel. The only good news was that few ex-Vibrators wound up in nowhere situations — John Ellis left to join Peter Gabriel's group, Tibbs split for Roxy Music and later, the aforementioned Ants. And besides, so long as Knox and Eddie were still around . . .

Or, at least, Eddie. By late 1978, he was the only original member left in the band, and even he was moonlighting with R&B monsters The Inmates. Working with former Electric Chairs guitarist Greg Van Cook and ex-Eater bassist Ian Woodcock, The Vibrators were about to start recording their third album when Epic dropped them.

The story could have ended there, but of course it didn't. Indeed, when The Vibrators returned in early 1980, Eddie and Woodcock, now accompanied by guitarists Phil Ram and Adrian Wyatt, came bearing one of their most powerful singles yet, the churning *Disco In Mosco*. Only then did they split up.

The original Vibrators line up reconvened in 1982, relaunching their new career in much the same way as they'd launched the old one, with a rerecording of *Baby Baby*. Since that time, The Vibrators have retained the same revolving door approach to membership that characterized them all along — Pat Collier quit in 1985 for a career in production, and John Ellis left and joined The Stranglers.

Mickie Owen, Ellis' replacement, was in turn succeeded by The Members' Nigel Bennett, in time for 1990's VICIOUS CIRCLE LP, and since then, such delights as 1993's THE POWER OF MONEY (a wryly titled collection of further re-makes) and the acoustic hits collection, UNPUNKED (1996.) Bennett himself then departed, to be replaced by latter-day UK Subber Darrell Bath. Another Sub, Gregor Kramer, would accompany Knox and Eddie on the 1999 Social Chaos tour. And so the story continues.

THE VIBRATORS DISCOGRAPHY
Singles 1976-80
- ○ *We Vibrate / Whips And Furs* (RAK 245, 1976)
- ○ *Pogo Dancing / The Pose* (RAK 246, 1976)
- ○ *Bad Time / No Heart* (RAK 253 [unreleased], 1976)
- ○ *Baby Baby / Into The Future* (Epic 5302, 1977)
- ○ *London Girls / Stiff Little Fingers* (live) (Epic 5565, 1977)
- ○ *Stiff Little Fingers / London Girls* (live) (Epic 5565DJ, 1977)
- ○ *Automatic Lover / Destroy* (Epic 6137, 1978)
- ○ *Judy Says / Pure Mania* (Epic 6393, 1978)
- ○ *Gimme Some Lovin' / Powercry* (Ratrace RAT 2, 1980)
- ○ *Disco In Mosco / Take A Chance* (Ratrace RAT 4, 1980)

Albums 1977-80
- ○ PURE MANIA (Epic 82097, 1977)
- ○ V2 (Epic 82497, 1978)
- ○ BATTERIES INCLUDED (CBS 3184007, 1980)
- ○ BBC RADIO ONE IN CONCERT (Windsong 036, 1977)
- ○ LIVE AT THE MARQUEE 1977 (Released Emotions REM 018, 1993)
- ○ DEMOS 76-77 (Dojo DOLE 102, 1994)
- ○ BBC PUNK SESSIONS (Captain Oi! AHOY 135, 2000)

◄ 5 ►
The Buzzcocks

The consummate UK singles group (who happened to make three great albums as well), the Buzzcocks were the first provincial (as in non-London) group to become involved in the gestating punk scene. Founders Pete Shelley and Howard Devoto (nee Trafford), meantime, were responsible for bringing The Sex Pistols to their hometown for shows in June and July of 1976. In fact, they formed their own outfit from members of the audience — bassist Steve Diggle was at the first gig and by the time of the second, the Buzzcocks were ready to open the show.

Diggle and drummer John Maher accompanied the duo at the Pistols' gig in July. The following month, The Buzzcocks made their London debut, opening for the Pistols and

The Clash at the Islington Screen On The Green. They also (inevitably) appeared at the 100 Club Punk festival in September, where Sniffin' Glue raved, "Their sound is very rough, very like the Pistols, but that guitar sound! It was a spitting, rasping monster."

The monster made it onto tape in October, when the Buzzcocks set about recording their first demos, sessions which would be split between the band's self-released debut single, the four song SPIRAL SCRATCH EP, and (later) the semi-exciting TIMES UP bootleg.

Released in January 1977, the EP's impressive run on the indy charts ended only when the group ran out of copies to sell. Demand lingered, however, and at one point SPIRAL SCRATCH ranked among the most sought-after of all first generation punk singles — only the Pistols' A&M 45, and The Clash's *Capital Radio* promo were guaranteed to raise temperatures higher. The EP was finally reissued in the summer of 1979, when it not only made the UK chart, it also brought a host of less welcome memories flooding back, of the day when Howard Devoto quit the Buzzcocks.

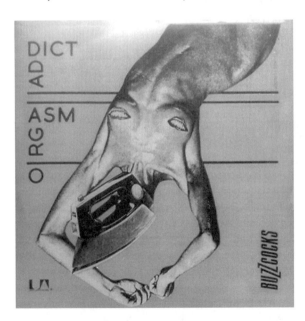

His departure made the front pages in the music press, much to the bemusement of a visiting Mick Jagger. He admitted to the NME, he read the story and "I went who leaves what?" That's when he knew he'd been out of Britain a long time. The Buzzcocks had just eleven gigs under their belt, but were already being described as one of the most significant new groups around. Devoto's defection could have crippled them, but The Buzzcocks rode out the storm with ease. With lead guitarist Shelley moving onto lead vocals (and rhythm guitar), Steve Diggle took over lead and early (brief) member

Garth Smith returned as bassist. The new line-up then went on the road with The Clash, an opening act on February 1977's White Riot tour; they also became regulars at the Roxy Club — when the venue was immortalized on wax that summer, The Buzzcocks were honored with two tracks on the album.

RAINBOW THEATRE
FINSBURY PARK   **304**

Asgard presents
BUZZCOCKS WITH GUESTS

at 8 p.m.

Saturday NOV 10

CIRCLE

Incl. VAT   **£2.50**

R 46

TO BE RETAINED   For conditions of sale see over

With that set acting as a high profile shop window, the Buzzcocks found record company interest reaching fever pitch. In August 1977, (the very day that Elvis Presley died), they signed to United Artists. Their debut single, *Orgasm Addict*, followed in November, but as the title implies, it was not the least controversial song in the band's repertoire. It was greeted with an immediate radio ban.

Smith quit on the eve of The Buzzcocks' first headlining tour — Steve Garvey replaced him and, with the exquisitely crafted *What Do I Get* and *I Don't Mind* having continued the group's run of crucial 45's, their debut album, ANOTHER MUSIC IN A DIFFERENT KITCHEN appeared in spring 1978.

The sharp pop of the singles was undiluted. The bulk of KITCHEN sparked with an effervescence which shocked even the band's admirers, while the masterful *16* and the percussive mindfuck of *Moving Away From The Pulsebeat* probed musical regions which set the Buzzcocks even further apart from the chasing pack — punks with a passion for prog rock, who would ever have guessed?

Further singles were machine gunned out. *Love You More*, widely reported as the shortest (one minute, 45 seconds) single ever made and *Ever Fallen In Love* (the band's biggest hit, No. 12) previewed the LOVE BITES album, while *Lipstick* slipped back into The Buzzcocks' past by resuscitating some vintage Shelley / Devoto riffery that the latter's own group, Magazine, had earlier employed for its debut single, *Shot By Both Sides*.

It was more than six months before The Buzzcocks were again sighted, with Steve Diggle's *Harmony In My Head*. It wasn't the best choice — admirable though they were, the guitarist's best songs always had a tendency to sound like Bad Company and *Harmony* was no exception. Still, fans nevertheless had cause to celebrate as the band's first trip to America was marked with SINGLES GOING STEADY, a collection of A- and B-sides which remains perhaps the definitive statement on the group's prowess. Few of the A-sides and none of the B's had appeared on album before, yet many of the latter, from the gratuitously controversial *Oh Shit*, through to the almost experimental *Something's Gone Wrong Again* and *Why Can't I Touch It*, stood alongside The Buzzcocks' finest works.

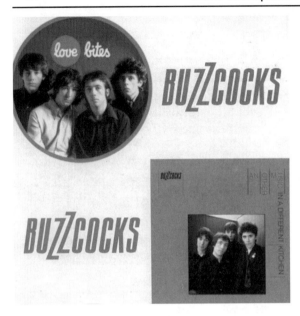

The TENSION album, meanwhile, proved as baffling as it was brilliant — side one wandered by without really getting going. Side two was dominated by a virtual suite of interconnected songs, ranging from the compulsively banal (*Hollow Inside*) to the absurdly ambitious (the seven minute *I Believe*) and ending with a few moments of transistor blasted static, through which ghosts of past singles could be made out. The schizophrenia was beginning to show.

A fall 1979 UK tour marked the end of The Buzzcocks. Although the group would continue on for close to another 18 months, it was clear that their own interest was waning — just three singles appeared during that span, oddly publicized with an "installment plan" tour, a handful of dates around each release. But the shows were sloppy, sometimes desultory and nobody was surprised when Shelley announced he'd quit the group. Nobody, that is, aside from his fellow 'cocks — when he went into the studio with producer Martin Rushent in the spring of 1981, they thought he was simply demoing new material for the next Buzzcocks album. Instead he emerged with his own solo debut, HOMOSAPIEN.

The Buzzcocks did reform, of course, reuniting in 1989 and, 11 years on, the Shelley / Diggle partnership has not only survived, it has thrived.

THE BUZZCOCKS DISCOGRAPHY
UK Singles
- SPIRAL SCRATCH EP: *Boredom / Friends Of Mine / Breakdown / Time's Up* (New Hormones ORG 1, 1977)
- *Orgasm Addict / Whatever Happened To . . .* (UA UP 36316, 1977)
- *What Do I Get? / Oh Shit!* (UA UP 36348, 1978)
- *I Don't Mind / Autonomy* (UA UP 36386, 1978)
- *Love You More / Noise Annoys* (UA UP 36433, 1978)
- *Ever Fallen In Love / Just Lust* (UA UP 36455, 1978)
- *Promises / Lipstick* (UA UP 36471, 1978)
- *Everybody's Happy Nowadays / Why Can't I Touch It?* (UA UP 36499, 1979)
- SPIRAL SCRATCH EP: *Boredom / Friends Of Mine / Breakdown / Time's Up* (New Hormones ORG 1, 1979)
- *You Say You Don't Love Me / Raison d'etre* (UA BP 316, 1979)
- *Are Everything / Girl From The Chainstore* (UA BP 365, 1980)
- *Strange Thing / Airwaves Dream* (UA BP 371, 1980)

- *Running Free / What Do You Know?* (UA BP 392, 1980)
- THE PEEL SESSION EP (1977): *What Do I Get? / Fast Cars / Pulsebeat* (Strange Fruit SFPS 44, 1988)

US Single
- *Believe / Something's Gone Wrong Again* (IRS I, 1979)

UK Albums
- ANOTHER MUSIC IN A DIFFERENT KITCHEN (UA UAG 30159, 1978)
- LOVE BITES (UA UAG 30197, 1978)
- A DIFFERENT KIND OF TENSION (UA UAG 30260, 1979)
- LIVE AT THE ROXY CLUB, APRIL 1977 (Absolutely Free LP 002, 1989)
- PRODUCT (5 LP boxed-set) (EMI PROD 1, 1989)
- THE PEEL SESSIONS (Strange Fruit SFRCD 104, 1990)
- OPERATORS MANUAL — BUZZCOCKS BEST (EMI 797534, 1991)
- LIVE AT THE ROXY, WC2 (compilation including Breakdown) (Receiver RR132, 1991)
- ENTERTAINING FRIENDS LIVE (EMI CDGOLD 1029, 1992)
- TIME'S UP (Dojo DLP 2, 1995)
- CHRONOLOGY (EMI LC 0542, 1997)

US Albums
- A DIFFERENT KIND OF TENSION (IRS SP 009, 1979)
- SINGLES GOING STEADY (IRS SP001, 1979)
- LEST WE FORGET — BUZZCOCKS LIVE (Roir A158, 1983)
- TEN ROIR YEARS (compilation including Ever Fallen in Love (live) (Roir A175, 1991)

⪡ 6 ⪢
Siouxsie & The Banshees

"If we'd thought this is like a job, and we're stuck with it, we never could have handled that." Drummer Budgie is adamant. "I don't think we're ever just ticking over, we've always had to fight for a lot of things and I think that's what's kept us going, telling people 'you're not gonna get away with that.'"

In amongst all the fuss and bother surrounding Siouxsie & the Banshees in the years since they "broke" America in the mid-late 1980's, and then broke up in 1996, it was very easy to forget just how far back their past stretched. The Banshees were twenty years old when they shattered — in protest, they insisted, at The Sex Pistols reunion (they later admitted the story wasn't true — but it really deserved to be.) Twenty years old and still incredulous that not only did they outlast virtually every one of their Brit-Punk contemporaries, they actually survived long enough to see the whole thing come around again.

Siouxsie (alongside bassist Steve Severin, the only member of the band to last the full course) reflected, "I think that maybe that's partly down to us, and partly down to . . . there was always a kind of naivete about the Banshees; it wasn't so cynical and marketed and desperately cash-kill oriented as some other groups. It also helped that we had that two year period without a record deal, so we were lucky to be allowed to play for two years, getting a fan base that way, rather than being sucked into the machinery at too early a stage."

The Banshees formed, she continues, "to fill in a gap at the 100 Club Punk Festival (in September, 1976.) We entered into the pure spirit of it, on the spur of the moment, forming a band to fill this slot then disbanding after it, one night only, taking the Andy Warhol idea to its extreme, and also the idea that now's now, and it's important — no future, no past."

SIOUXSIE AND THE BANSHEES ⭕ JOIN HANDS

They — Siouxsie, bassist Severin (then known as Steve Havoc), drummer Sid Vicious and future Beastly Cad / Adam and the Ants guitarist Marco Pirroni performed just one song, a storming, hypnotic version of *The Lord's Prayer*, shot through with a medley's worth of other iconic favorites, from *Twist And Shout* to *Knocking On Heaven's Door*.

That line-up split, but Sioux and Severin remained, recruiting guitarists John McKay and the shortlived PT Fenton and drummer Kenny Morris, and launching onto the road, spellbinding regulars at both the Roxy and the Vortex. Those earliest Banshees shows were astonishing, intense and spectacular. Siouxsie was skin and bone in black and kohl, a commanding presence swinging slow-mo from the microphone through the most scarifying collection of songs on show — *Carcass, Bad Shape, Switch, Helter Skelter* and *Metal Postcard.* What became the group's debut album, 1978's THE SCREAM, took shape on shitty stages round Britain, and its follow-up, JOIN HANDS, as well. Uniquely, the Banshees mapped out their future before they'd even had a chance to start recording their past.

But if they didn't make records, what did they do? Why, they spraypainted their existence on record company walls, of course. Every morning, someone would turn up for work to find SIGN THE BANSHEES NOW! scrawled across the building. None of them did. "CBS's walls, EMI's walls, Island, Polydor, they all got it. But we weren't really involved in that." Siouxsie sounds, surprisingly, horrified. "We didn't have the time to do that. It was actually a big fan of ours who'd probably be really embarrassed if he knew I told you, 'no no no!' It was actually Les Mills who went on to manage the Furs. He had blonde hair, a leather jacket and studs, with SIOUXSIE on it. For those two years he was pretty obsessive about it, then he got his own group together."

Talk that the band was about to sign to the BBC's own record label (at the prompting of devoted supporter John Peel) was finally canned when Polydor moved in for the group, scoring an instant hit with *Hong Kong Garden*, then finally following through with THE SCREAM.

The brittle, swirling *Staircase* followed, and the megalithic JOIN HANDS. Then, just as it seemed that the band was bound for instant glory — and just four nights into their latest tour, McKay and Morris walked out. The evening's support group, The Cure, played an elongated set in the headliners' absence — Siouxsie and Severin then joined them on stage for a colossal *Lord's Prayer* finale.

Four subsequent shows were cancelled, but on September 18, 1979, less than two weeks after the split, the Banshees were back to full strength and on the road again. Drums now were handled by former Big In Japan / Slits stickman Budgie, and guitar duties fell to Robert Smith, still hot and sweaty from the Cure's own opening slot. He would give way to Magazine's John McGeogh after the tour (then return briefly to replace McGeogh in 1982.)

1980 dawned, then, not only with a new Banshees line-up, but a new sound as well. Forever flirting on the edge of a peculiar, particular, musical darkness, the Banshees now leaped wholeheartedly into it. And though they did not, as some mealy-mouthed miseries liked to moan, abandon punk rock for goth, they defined the division all the same.

SIOUXSIE & THE BANSHEES DISCOGRAPHY
UK Singles 1978-79
- *Hong Kong Garden / Voices* (Polydor 2059 052, 1978)
- *The Staircase (Mystery) / 20th Century Boy* (Polydor POSP 9, 1979)
- *Playground Twist / Pull To Bits* (Polydor POSP 59, 1979)
- *Mittageisen / Love In A Void* (Polydor 2059 151, 1979)
- THE PEEL SESSION EP: *Love In A Void / Mirage / Metal Postcard / Suburban Relapse* (Strange Fruit SFPS 012, 1987)
- THE PEEL SESSION EP: *Hong Kong Garden / Overground / Carcase / Helter Skelter* (Strange Fruit SFPS 066, 1988)

US Singles 1978-79
- *Hong Kong Garden / Overground* (Polydor, 1978)

UK Albums 1978-79
- THE SCREAM (Polydor POLD 5009, 1978)
- JOIN HANDS (Polydor POLD 5024, 1979)
- ONCE UPON A TIME (compilation) (Polydor POLS 1056, 1981)

US Albums 1978-79
- THE SCREAM (Polydor 6207, 1978)

◄ 7 ►
Subway Sect

Vic Godard, a native of the London suburb of Mortlake, put Subway Sect together during the summer of 1976, centering it around the coterie of friends with whom he went to Sex Pistols shows. Rehearsing at The Clash's generously loaned space, Subway Sect took their name from their principle source of income, busking outside Hammersmith underground station.

The band made their live debut on 20 September, 1976 at — where else? — the 100 Club Punk festival, the first group to take the stage that night, with a line-up of Godard, Paul Myers (bass), Robert Miller (guitar) and Paul Smith (drums.) Smith had been playing his instrument for just five weeks at that point, with only one of those spent with his cohorts.

It was a fascinating first performance. "[They] had all the intellectual wimpeys cringing in horror and yapping about how the band couldn't play, ect.," reported Sniffin' Glue fanzine. "I loved 'em. They chew gum onstage and look vacant. The four songs (*No Love* was the first one) they did were great."

Godard himself remarked, "I thought I wasn't going to like going onstage, but when you get up there it's just like you're one of the audience. I always take the attitude that we're practicing in front of a load of people. So it seems to me, we do exactly the same when we're practicing as when we play live. There's only one difference — when we practice and we do something wrong, we stop, but when we play live we just carry on." He added, apropos of nothing, that he still wanted to dribble when he was 25.

The 100 Club audience was torn between love (the punks) and hate (the rest), but the group seemed to put every issue beyond doubt at the conclusion of the set. "We're splitting up now," Godard announced. "The end."

He was lying. For the next two months or so, the Sect were a fitful fixture on the live circuit, hampered more by the paucity of suitable venues than any lack of intention on their part. Their sets remained short — of one gig, at a wedding, Godard explained, "We did *Steppin' Stone* and a couple of ones I'd written. We did a complete noise first — that's what made everybody walk out — where everyone smashed guitars around. I just chanted some poetry over it."

In January, 1977, drummer Mark Laff took over from Smith and, in this form, the Sect opened for The Clash at the Harlesden Roxy, making such an impression that they were promptly invited onto the headliners' forthcoming White Riot UK tour. Their first European assault followed and, though Mark Laff was lured away by Generation X in May, new drummer Bob Ward slotted effortlessly in, and the Sect raved on.

Despite their prowess, it was close to another year before the group finally cut a single — Warm Records had expressed interest during 1977, but finally the band linked with Clash manager Bernie Rhodes' Braik label for *Nobody Scared* (first aired at the 100 Club show) in March, 1978. To back it up, Sect visited France to warm-up for their forthcoming UK tour.

A wholesale split sundered the group that summer, as Rhodes sacked everybody but Godard and Ward. John Britten (guitar), Colin Scott (bass) and Steve Atkinson (keyboards) joined and in October, following months of inactivity, Subway Sect toured Britain with The Buzzcocks. *Ambition*, a single taped earlier in the year, joined them on display the following month but, though there was some excited talk of an album, it fizzled out. It would be 1996 before the full studio legacy of the classic Sect finally made it out, on the WE OPPOSE ALL ROCK'N'ROLL collection. The band themselves crumbled in late 1978.

After abortive one-off unions with singer Virginia Astley and GREAT ROCK'N'ROLL SWINDLE bit part players the Black Arabs (both featured on WE OPPOSE), Godard reconvened Subway Sect in 1980 with a new line-up and a very different attitude, experimenting with new vocal and musical styles and edging close to what history now recalls as the New Romantic movement. Once when Godard insisted the Sect "opposed all rock'n'roll," it was because they had a viable alternative. And it wasn't lounge lizard crooning.

SUBWAY SECT PUNK DISCOGRAPHY
Singles
- *Nobody's Scared / Don't Spit On It* (Braik BRS 01, 1978)
- *Ambition / A Different Story* (Rough Trade 7, 1978)

Album
- WE OPPOSE ALL ROCK'N'ROLL (Overground 53, 1996)

≪ Part Two ≫
– Live At The Roxy –

If any single site could epitomize punk, it was the Roxy. After a couple of try-outs shortly before Christmas, the club was opened on January 1, 1977, in Neal Street, Covent Garden, by Generation X manager Andy Czezowski. Essentially borrowing Malcolm McLaren's vision of a punks-only club, Czezowski forged a venue which, though it swiftly developed into a cliché of its own, did much to establish the initial unity of punk (Brian James numbers The Damned's first few shows there among his favorites ever) while DJ Don Letts' presence contributed much to the eventual twinning of punk and reggae, two rebel musics in it together.

"When the Roxy started," Letts explained, "there were literally no punk records to play ... so I had to play something I liked, which was reggae. I guess I did turn a few people on to it. The crowd wanted to hear more reggae. We turned each other on through our different cultures."

The Roxy served another purpose, however — as a training ground for new acts. Many of the groups making their Roxy debuts had barely played more than a show or two in their lives, but it's a mark of the club's success that a lot of them went on to considerably greater things.

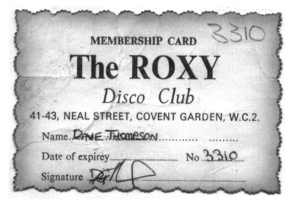

Czezowski departed the scene in late April, around the same time as the now-legendary LIVE AT THE ROXY, LONDON, WC2 compilation was recorded. The venue continued on, but his vision and passion were as integral to the club's well-being as the groups themselves. Increasingly lowly "headline" attractions chased away some of the audience. The presence of another new venue, the Vortex, lured away others. Between January and April, 1979, the Roxy was arguably instrumental in cementing the fame of some 20 different bands. Between May and December, only the U.K. Subs truly profited from its existence.

CLASSIC ROXY CONCERTS – THE FIRST 100 DAYS

dates are largely drawn from contemporary memorabilia, advertising etc and may not be 100% accurate. Readers with additional information are invited to contact the publishers.

December 1976
- 14 Generation X
- 15 The Heartbreakers
- 21 Siouxsie & The Banshees, Generation X

January 1977
- 1   The Clash, The Heartbreakers
- 13 Eater
- 14 The Damned
- 15 Generation X, The Adverts
- 17 Eater, The Damned
- 19 Slaughter & The Dogs, The Adverts
- 24 The Damned
- 27 The Vibrators, The Outsiders, The Drones
- 29 Generation X, Penetration
- 31 The Damned

February 1977
- 3   Eater, Johnny Moped
- 4   Chelsea, Cocksparra
- 5   The Cortinas, Masterswitch

- 6 The Adverts
- 7 The Damned
- 9 The Vibrators, The Rejects
- 10 Little Village ("funky latin salsa sound"!)
- 11 The Jam, The Lurkers
- 12 Slaughter & The Dogs, Beastly Cads
- 14 The Damned, The Adverts
- 16 The Vibrators, GBH
- 19 The Cortinas, The Bombers
- 21 The Damned, Johnny Moped
- 23 Slaughter & The Dogs
- 24 Wire, Jam, The Rejects
- 25 The Drones
- 28 The Damned, The Adverts

March 1977

- 2 The Heartbreakers
- 3 Cherry Vanilla and the Police
- 4 Wayne County, The Adverts
- 11 Chelsea, X-Ray Spex, The Drones
- 12 Shakin Streets, The Zips
- 15 The Jam, The Adverts
- 16 The Boys, Wire
- 17 Eater, The Lurkers
- 18 Slaughter & The Dogs, Johnny Moped
- 19 The Models (+ Cortinas, Beastly Cads?)
- 22 The Jam, The Rejects
- 23 Eater, Sham 69
- 24 The Boys, Kubie & The Rats
- 25 Chelsea, The Adverts
- 26 Siouxsie & The Banshees, The Slits
- 29 The Stranglers (?)
- 31 The Damned, Johnny Moped
- unknown date: The Only Ones

April 1977

- 1 The Buzzcocks, Wire
- 2 Wire
- 9 Generation X, Penetration
- 15 The Cortinas, The Models
- 16 Wire, Johnny Moped, X-Ray Spex, Smak, The Buzzcocks
- 18 Wayne County, The Adverts
- 22 Slaughter & The Dogs, The Lurkers

≪ **8** ≫
The Adverts

TV Smith was the only member of The Adverts with any prior musical experience, a self-released album with his college-days group Sleaze in 1975, but it never really showed. Bassist Gaye Advert learned to play as the band rehearsed, borne along as much by enthusiasm as musical ability. Laurie Driver, in Smith's own words, "stumbled into an audition one day and pretended to play drums, so we hired him." And guitarist Howard Pickup, while a skilled musician, had never played anywhere more demanding than a folk club.

But an early rehearsal tape, dating from the tail end of 1976, shows that Smith's singular vision had indeed found the ideal conspirators: Gaye's bass pounds through the opening *One Chord Wonders*; Driver's drums sound like dustbins across *New Boys*; and, all the while, Pickup's tight, economical guitar is probing the edges of the songs, looking for a way out.

When Smith and Advert arrived in London in the summer of 1976, they were surprised to find a whole scene percolating, making precisely the kind of music they had dreamed of in their native Devon. But really, nobody would make music like The Adverts and nobody ever has. In terms of lyric, delivery, commitment and courage, they were, and they remain, the finest British group of the late 1970's.

The Adverts made their live debut at the Roxy on January 15, 1977, supporting Generation X. The headliners' drummer, John Towe, worked in the same West End music store as Pickup and had promised to help the new band get gigs. Four days later, The Adverts returned to the venue, opening for Slaughter And The Dogs' maiden capital appearance, and immediately they began making friends.

NME scribe, Miles would go on to produce The Adverts' third single. Brian James of The Damned promised the group both live shows and an introduction to his record label. And publishing magnate Michael Dempsey, lured down to the Roxy because "anything that the Daily Express hated so much must have had something going for it," became the group's manager.

Talking in 1979, Dempsey himself recalled, "the first time I went to the Roxy I saw The Damned, the second time it was The Adverts. It could only have been their second or third gig ever, but I thought they were dynamic, especially Tim's lyrics."

"The thing with The Adverts, they were always being lumped in with the rest of the No Future brigade, but they were taking a far more realistic view of things. Tim might have believed in the ideals of the punk thing, but he also understood its limitations, which is something that very few people did, especially at that time. While everyone else was celebrating how 'different' they were, how outrageous, Tim was saying 'so what?', asking them what they were trying to prove. While they were challenging the establishment, he was challenging the challengers."

One of the first contracts to come under Dempsey's scrutiny was the deal being offered by Stiff Records. True to his word, Brian James had put the company onto the group, and when Stiff supremo Jake Riviera caught the group at the Roxy (where else?), he shared James' enthusiasm.

In the studio with former Pink Fairies guitarist Larry Wallis, The Adverts put down two of their strongest numbers, both vaguely autobiographical, *One Chord Wonders* and *Quickstep*. It was a convincing debut, a headlong rush of energy which Sounds made their Single of the Week, Melody Maker "recommended," and the NME called "mundane rock music from New Wave flotsam and jetsam . . . almost unbelievably boring." Obviously somebody wasn't paying attention that week.

The single was in the shops in April, and the band was on the road, a thirty three date tour supporting The Damned, with Stiff forking out for full page ads in the music press to let everyone know that "The Damned can now play three chords, The Adverts can play one. Hear all four at . . ." Despite such mockery, The Adverts finished the tour teetering on what even the NME now acknowledged was "the edge of a great step forward."

On April 25, The Adverts made their debut on BBC Radio 1 disc jockey John Peel's nightly show, recording the five track session which would, a full decade later, become one of the flagship releases in Strange Fruit's PEEL SESSIONS series. If anybody required evidence of just how far the group had progressed in the four months since their debut, this was it. And if they needed further proof, that was at hand too.

In June, Harvest released what they described as "a document of those halcyon days down at the Roxy," the eight band live showcase LIVE AT THE ROXY, LONDON WC2. Captured in what could, accurately if a little generously, be described as their natural environment, Wire, X Ray Spex, The Buzzcocks and Johnny Moped slammed through a

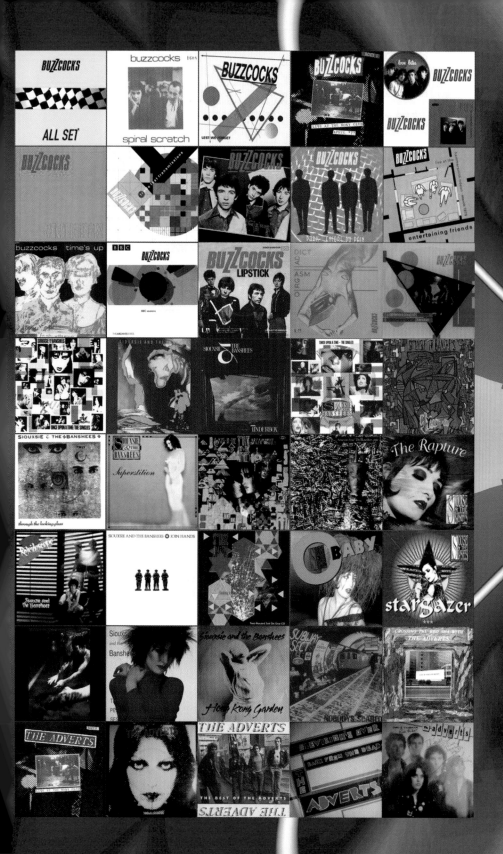

Billy Idol, Cow Palace, San Francisco, CA 1984
copyright Phil Anderson / KAOS2000 Magazine

highlight or two of their live set, the ramshackle rattle of tinny amps and cheapo guitars and, as ramshackle and rattling as any of them, The Adverts closed side one with *Bored Teenagers*. It was recorded at their third ever Roxy appearance and hit the streets just as the group prepared to start recording its second single.

Several record companies had moved in for The Adverts' signature — having initially despised punk rock, the British music industry now couldn't get enough, with every label head demanding his own safety-pinned signing. Polydor snagged The Jam, CBS got The Clash, Virgin landed the Pistols, UA grabbed The Stranglers . . . The Adverts went to Anchor, the British arm of ABC.

The deal was the standard one single with options offering, but that suited The Adverts as much as it did the company accountants — Dempsey had no doubt that a handful of hits was all it would take to push the band into the big league. They could worry about long term contracts later. Neither was his faith misplaced. Retaining Larry Wallis as producer, the group got to work on *Gary Gilmore's Eyes*, and a studio stab at *Bored Teenagers*.

Truly one of the most delectably macabre subjects ever picked for pop immortality, *Gary Gilmore's Eyes* was inspired by American Death Row denizen Gilmore's insistence that following his execution, his eyes be donated to medical science for transplant ("I don't think the heart will be any good.") Smith, as one does, then began wondering about the eyes' recipient and what delights might be in store for him. It was only ironic, then, that the whole time the single was on the British chart, "the BBC spelt Gilmore wrong, so there were all these people thinking that I was singing about a sportsman" — Gary Gilmour was a star of the English cricket team.

"The sickest and cleverest record to come out of the New Wave: Single of the Week," proclaimed Sounds. "Idea of the week, if not the performance," championed NME. And in the record stores, sales of the 45 leaped from a respectable 3,000 a day to a staggering 10,000 after Gaye spent her 21st birthday watching herself on TOP OF THE POPS. Four days later, *Gary Gilmore's Eyes* burst into the chart. It finally peaked at No. 18.

Gary Gilmore's Eyes was not, of course, an unexpected hit. The past eight months had seen The Adverts gigging incessantly, setting the pattern for the remainder of their career and establishing a reputation second to none throughout provincial England. Almost alone of the first division New Wave groups, The Adverts proved totally unafraid of forsaking the comforts of the London punk circuit for the rigors of perpetual touring — in their own right and, during September, opening for Iggy Pop, as they awaited the release of their third single, *Safety In Numbers*. No wonder Rat Scabies, in his last interview before quitting The Damned, mourned, "even the fucking Adverts are bigger than us now!"

But were they as big as they should have been? Media interest from *Gary Gilmore's Eyes* was enough to push the new single to the edge of the Top 75, but absolutely inexplicably, a few weeks of hopeful Bubbling Under gave way to oblivion.

The group spent November 1977 recording their debut album, CROSSING THE RED SEA WITH THE ADVERTS. The new year then brought their fourth single, *No Time To Be 21* (released through Bright Records, a newly formed offshoot of Anchor.) The album followed, a devastating debut even if more than a quarter of its weight was taken up with previously released (albeit newly rerecorded) material. Based exclusively around the band's live set, the album, like the show, closed with *Great British Mistake*, a genuine tour de force and still one of Smith's most dynamic creations. Lyrically, it looked at the nation's need to find a scapegoat for everything. Musically, it set a jarring, staccato pace which refused to let up for a moment. When NME critic Charles Shaar Murray questioned whether The Adverts could ever become as "ramshackle and unmusical in as exciting a manner as the Velvet Underground," this was his answer, a soaring feedback extravaganza pinned down by bass and drums which brought the song to its conclusion, and the audience to its knees.

In years to come, CROSSING THE RED SEA was to be spoken of in the terms of hushed reverence elsewhere reserved for the greatest debut albums of our time, Roxy Music and Patti Smith, the classics which only the terminally cloth-eared can dispute. In 1978, however, even with the full weight of the music press and another sell-out British tour behind it, the album sank almost without trace. It spent just one week in the Top 40, trailing in the slipstream of *No Time To Be 21*'s Top 50 success, then fell away.

The Adverts were on the road constantly through the beginning of 1978, a colossal outing which would keep them occupied until March, with another Roundhouse headliner midway through. It was to prove an eventful excursion. Early into the Irish leg of the tour, Laurie Driver succumbed to hepatitis. Two live shows were cancelled (although a roadie stood in for the group's RTE television debut), and The Adverts returned to London with just five days to find a replacement. They opted for John Towe, the ex-Chelsea and Generation X drummer whose own latest band, Rage, supported The Adverts through much of their November 1977 tour. He, in turn, quit in March, at the end of the tour, to be replaced by ex-Maniacs drummer Rod Latter, one of two musicians who braved a London blizzard to attend the audition. "The other guy had long hair and a beard," Latter recalled. "He was every bit as good as me. I think I got through on image."

Thus began a new era of non-stop gigging, this time with an emphasis on the continent, a virgin territory so far as The Adverts were concerned. Another beckoning pasture was America. Dempsey was telling everyone that his group was going to be bigger than Beatlemania in the States, although he would probably have settled simply for a record deal. RED SEA was one of the stars of the import scene through early 1978, but the intellectual giants at ABC didn't pay it an iota of attention. Decrying the importance of the punk upheaval on the British scene as just that, an isolated upheaval in a market whose day had already come and gone, ABC pronounced that punk would never impact on American tastes and refused outright to even consider giving RED SEA a Stateside release. By the early summer of 1978, The Adverts had quit Anchor.

MUSIC MACHINE

Camden High Street
Off Mornington Cres. Tube Station
Tele 387-0428-9

£1·50 adm. with this ticket.

SATURDAY 23rd JUNE

Adverts

PLUS SUPPORT

Music. Food. Bars. Dancing. 8pm. 2am. Min Age 18yrs
Admission Without This Ticket £2.
Management Reserve The Right Of Admission

Rumors flew concerning a short season at CBGBs. Recording sessions with what Dempsey described as "a heavyweight American producer" were also mooted. Ultimately, however, both plans were quietly forgotten and The Adverts instead began diligently rehearsing a new set, to be unleashed at two London Marquee gigs in August. Indeed, by the time The Adverts went to Germany in early September, almost half the set comprised fresh songs.

Five of the new songs were included in the band's next John Peel session on September 11, 1978. Three of them also made it onto the big screen when The Adverts took the headline role in German director Wolfgang Buld's acclaimed television movie BRENNEDE LANGAWEILE (BURNING BOREDOM.)

Returning home, The Adverts signed the worldwide deal they had been hankering after, pledging themselves to RCA — who immediately sacked the person responsible and sent the group into the studio to see what they could come up with. They responded with another mighty 45, *Television's Over* — produced, to the astonishment of everyone who read the credits, by Tom Newman, best known for his work with Mike Oldfield.

Although it ranked among RCA's biggest selling singles of the season, *Television's Over* did not come within sniffing distance of the chart. Still, its performance was sufficient to convince RCA that they'd made a wise signing after all and, early in 1979, the band was despatched to the palatial Manor Studios, with Newman again in tow, to begin work on their second album. From there, with four tracks in the can, the proceedings shifted to the Barge, a floating studio on London's Regents Canal.

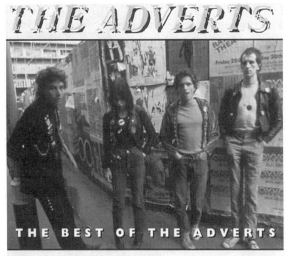

CAST OF THOUSANDS never threatened to be just another punk rock record. Although the group's live performance remained as fiery as ever, Smith was opening the group's sound to all manner of outside opportunities, including augmenting the line-up with keyboards. The Doctors Of Madness' Richard Strange handled synth on what would become the new album's title track (Strange and Smith also wrote a number of songs together, the *Back From The Dead* B-side among them), before Newman brought in another Mike Oldfield sideman, Tim Cross.

The Adverts' T.V. Smith

The Adverts

With another single in the stores, the change-of-pace *My Place*, The Adverts played a handful of shows during the summer, intended to keep them ticking over until a full tour planned for the fall. However, the departures of first Pickup, then Latter, ensured that by the time the outing got underway, the core of Smith, Advert and the now-permanent Cross was joined by session guitarist Paul Martinez and his brother, Rick.

In fact, the group had broken up, continuing on only to fill sundry contractual obligations, in turn ensuring that RCA went ahead with the album release. As it turned out, the band had already played its final show, at Slough College on October 27, 1979, before CAST OF THOUSANDS hit the streets

"There are advantages in going out with a whimper when everyone looks upon you as being really shit," Smith reflected, "although I'd have loved to go out with a really big tour. It all came down to money, though, and RCA's lack of giving us any. If I look back on the last few years, now I can see it as a two or three year thing. The Adverts were continually standing on the outside, and seeing what they could do. But while it was still going, everything was perfect as far as I was concerned. People were really insulting about Gaye's playing, but on the second album and the last tour, she was playing really well. I mean, it's pointless to compare her with Jack Bruce, but she was right for The Adverts, and for what we were doing."

Now they weren't doing anything at all. Gaye, after briefly contemplating a solo career, ultimately decided to quit the music industry altogether. Today, she works in local government. Pickup, Driver, Towe and Latter, too, fled the field (Pickup died in 1997), while Cross returned to session work. Only Smith himself has continued pursuing the chimera which The Adverts unleashed, with the Explorers and Cheap, and now, solo.

THE ADVERTS DISCOGRAPHY
UK Singles
- ○ *One Chord Wonders / Quickstep* (Stiff BUY BUY 13, 1977)
- ○ *Gary Gilmore's Eyes / Bored Teenagers* (Anchor ANC 1043, 1977)
- ○ *Safety In Numbers / We Who Wait* (Anchor ANC 1047, 1977)
- ○ *No Time To Be 21 / New Day Dawning* (Bright BR 1, 1978)
- ○ *Television's Over / Back From The Dead* (RCA PB 5128, 1978)
- ○ *My Place / New Church* (live) (RCA PB 5160, 1979)
- ○ *Cast Of Thousands / I Will Walk You Home* (RCA PB 5160, 1979)
- ○ *Gary Gilmore's Eyes* (unreleased version) / *We Who Wait / New Day Dawning* (Bright BULB 1, 1983)
- ○ THE PEEL SESSIONS EP: (five tracks) (Strange Fruit SFPS 34, 1987)

UK Albums
- ○ CROSSING THE RED SEA WITH THE ADVERTS (Bright BRL 2001, 1978)
- ○ CAST OF THOUSANDS (RCA PL 25246, 1979)
- ○ LIVE AT THE ROXY (Receiver RRCD 136, 1990)
- ○ LIVE AND LOUD (Link CD 159, 1992)
- ○ THE SINGLES COLLECTION (Anagram CDPUNK 95, 1997)
- ○ CROSSING THE RED SEA (Castle ESMCD 451, 1997)

○ THE WONDERS DON'T CARE — THE COMPLETE RADIO RECORDINGS
(Burning Airlines PILOT 3, 1997)
○ CAST OF THOUSANDS (Anagram CDPUNK 102, 1998)
○ THE BEST OF THE ADVERTS (Anagram CDPUNK 107, 1998)

◄ 9 ►
The Boys

Matt Dangerfield and Norwegian-born pianist Casino Steel, founding members of the Hollywood Brats and early participants in the London SS, linked up with Kid Reid, Jack Black and John Plain in June, 1976. Their directive was simple: to create hard-edged pop music with enough bite to pass the burgeoning punk standards, but enough melody to get by in the mainstream. It says much for their ambition that, within two years, the so-called "power pop" explosion owed its every ounce of impetus to The Boys' frantic majesty.

It was to be a year before The Boys found a recording contract, a year during which their reputation soared and grown men found themselves incapable of resisting the group's cut'n'thrust capering. By the end of 1977, Zig Zag's Alan Anger was marvelling, "The Boys ... have stood by and watched the demise of The Sex Pistols and Damned, as well as the rise of The Clash, Jam and Rezillos. Yet they know that they have a perfect rock / pop formula and it's too bad if the general UK public cannot see the greatness of the group."

NEMS, a small label continually bedeviled by both artistic and distribution setbacks, adopted The Boys during the spring of '77 and, in April, their first, great, single appeared. *I Don't Care* was an instant alternative chart topper. By early 1978, The Boys' continued domination of the punk / new wave charts was to be acknowledged in the title of their second album, ALTERNATIVE CHARTBUSTERS. In the meantime, however, they slogged round the same circuit as every other bugger, winning over even the most cynical crowd on the night, but never translating their live popularity to the mainstream.

Thus *First Time*, in July, passed all but the punk cognoscenti by and, in November, The Boys' eponymous debut album (recorded in just two days) all but went the same way. One week at No. 50 is not the stuff from which dreams are made, after all. Small wonder, then, that drummer Black swore he'd given up watching TV pop programs, "because it makes me sick seeing bands who couldn't lick our boots on there every week." Maybe, he conceded, it was too much to expect The Boys to soar to the toppermost of the poppermost, at a time when even The Buzzcocks, The

Ramones and The Jam, the bands with which their vision could most accurately be aligned, were still struggling around the butt-end of the chart. But some sort of breakthrough would have been nice.

Christmas brought the first of the group's annual transmogrifications into the Yobs, a foul-mouthed party band that delighted in reinventing sundry Yuletime favorites (they kicked off with Chuck Berry's *Run Rudolph Run*), while early 1978 saw ALTERNATIVE CHARTBUSTERS and the devastating *Brickfield Nights* single reinforce The Boys' buzzsaw brilliance, blistered breakneck guitar leads underpinning classic, contagious melodies.

Quitting NEMS with their next album already half finished, The Boys moved to Safari and started again, emerging with TO HELL WITH THE BOYS, their finest album yet. Highlighted by a furious version of the classical *Sabre Dance* and a devastating new single, *Kamikaze*, it was released in October 1979, just as The Boys joined the latest Ramones tour. The sight of sundry Boys joining da bruddahs on stage for *Baby I Love You* remains a precious memory.

But still The Boys' records weren't selling and confidence was fading fast. Plain left for The

The Boys

Lurkers, Steel quit to be replaced by former X-Ray Spex saxophonist Rudi and the band cut their fourth album, BOYS ONLY, already aware that its title summed up its potential market as much as anything else. Reid was next to leave in March 1981. With ex-Lurker Howard Wall stepping into the breach, The Boys cut one final single, *Woch Woch Woch*, then broke up.

The Boys were perhaps punk's most lachrymose casualty. They could — indeed, should — have been enormous. Certainly they were one of the finest live acts around, but still they were to languish in comparative obscurity. Even worse, when their debut album was reissued on CD, it arrived with a sticker on the front proclaiming the involvement of 80's AOR superstar John Waite — a claim which even Waite admits has absolutely no grounding in reality. More recent reissues have redressed the balance (or at least, dumped the sticker), but even they don't have too much to brag about. Just a host of great songs, an arsenal of killer hooks, and too many lost opportunities to count.

THE BOYS DISCOGRAPHY

UK Singles
- *I Don't Care / Soda Pressing* (NEM 102, 1977)
- *First Time / Whatcha Gonna Do / Turning Grey* (NEM 111, 1977)
- *Brickfield Nights / Teacher's Pet* (NEM 116, 1978)
- *Kamikaze / Bad Days* (Safari SAFE 21, 1979)
- *Terminal Love / I Love Me* (Safari SAFE 23, 1980)
- *You Better Move On / Schoolgirls* (Safari SAFE 27, 1980)
- *Weekend / Cool* (Safari SAFE 31, 1980)
- *Let It Rain / Lucy Lucy* (Safari SAFE 33, 1980)
- *Woch Woch Woch / One Way* (Parole, 1981)

UK Albums
- THE BOYS (NEM NEL 6001, 1977)
- ALTERNATIVE CHARTBUSTERS (NEM NEL 6015, 1978)
- TO HELL WITH THE BOYS (Safari 12BOYS, 1979)
- BOYS ONLY (Safari BOYS 4, 1980)
- LIVE AT THE ROXY (Link CLINK 4, 1991)
- BBC RADIO ONE IN CONCERT (Windsong, 1993)

○ ORIGINAL MIXES (Revolution, 1996)
○ COMPLETE PUNK SINGLES COLLECTION (Anagram CDPUNK 85, 1997)
○ THE BOYS (Captain Oi Ahoy CD 101, 1999)
○ ALTERNATIVE CHARTBUSTERS (Captain Oi Ahoy CD 104, 1999)

◄ **10** ►
Chelsea

When Gene October placed an ad in Melody Maker, seeking musicians to join him in a new group, he could have had no idea what he was unleashing. Beginning that summer of 1976, however, Chelsea emerged as one of the longest lived, and alternately most exciting and most infuriating, of all the first generation punk groups. Not only that, but they were also responsible for bringing together another coterie of the movement's prime movers, when October's ad was answered by a philosophy student named William "Billy Idol" Broad, former London SS bassist Tony James, and drummer John Towe.

October himself had been on the verge of forming a teenybop group called Love And Kisses when he became aware of punk. Immediately he changed course and was now looking for group members young, loud and snotty enough to elevate him to stardom in this latest wave.

With Idol on guitar, October's Chelsea debuted at the London ICA on October 13, 1976, supporting Throbbing Gristle's PROSTITUTE art exhibition and playing behind a stripper named Shelley. Their set was unremarkable, eleven songs centering around the first few Rolling Stones albums. However, the break up of this original line-up in November was the cue for October to unleash a string of would-be classic singles, beginning with the almighty *Right To Work*.

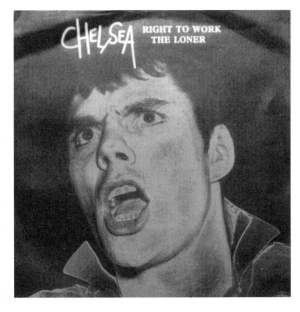

Immediately after the split, October told Mark P of Sniffin' Glue that he would "bounce back." P however, "never expected him to come up with another group so soon. This new Chelsea have a completely different way of thinking than the original mob." Bob Jessie (bass), Marti Stacey (guitar) and Carey Fortune (drums)

were the new Chelsea, debuting at the Roxy supporting The Clash in January 1977.

Another early, impressive show was at the Hope And Anchor, filmed and divided into two sets. The first went great, the second, however, was cancelled after a gang of Teddy Boys descended upon the place. The band packed up and headed off to the safer pastures of the Roxy, where they played yet another full set. Enthused Mark P, "now that's what rock's all about, getting up and playing. Chelsea would gig every night if they could, energy is what they've definitely got."

Staying power, however, was not. By March 1977, following a chain reaction of shifts and changes, Fortune alone remained on board as teenage wizard James Stevenson came in on guitar and Henry Badowski on bass. "I've got a friend who works in Capital radio, called Nicky Horne," October explained. "I walked up to Capital one day to try and get 'em to play *White Riot.* We got chatting and I told him I needed a bass player and there was this guy who answers the phones. 'Oh,' he says, 'I'm a bass player.' He auditioned, we liked him and that was that."

It was this line up that cut what remains perhaps Chelsea's finest, certainly their most potent, record, *Right To Work.* "Fuck the unions," October snarled. "Your father worked on this dock, you'll work on this dock. If you don't sign with the fucking union, you don't get the job." *The Loner,* the B-side, was "more personal to me, but also I reckon there's a lot of loners. A lot of kids who die when they're 14, 15 . . . just die, no feelings. I personally died a long time ago."

It was this kind of undiluted didacticism which, initially, put a lot of people off the band, but

October didn't care. "I hope to instigate something if I can. I wanna take [punk] away from the rough side that it's got and I wanna add a bit of smoothness to it, a bit of polish, a bit of style. There's too many of these punk groups being looked on as thickos. I haven't even got my message over. One gets accused of being a poseur, one gets accused of writing stuff cos that's the thing to write about. I've had all that."

Chelsea played every club that would take them, a frantic roaring behemoth which may not have won any awards for finesse, but whose commitment could never be doubted. What was uncertain was their future. Even before the release of their second single, *High Rise Living*, Badowski quit to play sax for Wreckless Eric. Simon Vitesse replaced him and the band recorded *Urban Kids* for inclusion in the Derek Jarman movie, JUBILEE. By September, however, Chelsea had split up, only for January 1978 to bring a new line-up: October, Stevenson, Dave Martin (guitar), Jeff Miles (bass) and Chris Bashford (drums.)

A new version of *Urban Kids* debuted the group on vinyl and, though it would be close to another year before they released their first album, on stage, in front of one of the most partisan audiences of the era, they were kings of the world. It was only when one opened the UK music press that one got a taste of the sheer hostility which Chelsea attracted.

The problem Chelsea was experiencing was one of "too little, too late." Having ranked among the first wave of punk, but refusing to compromise the ideals which sparked that initial explosion, Chelsea already seemed a band out of time. Sleeping uncomfortably alongside second, even third generation groups, they were, of course, still adored by the punks who came to see them. But they were also well aware that those punks were a far cry from the ones they had so entertained during their earliest days.

This malaise only slightly affected the CHELSEA album, but traced through the progression of singles that made up ALTERNATIVE HITS, the singles-only compilation which arrived early in 1981, it was glaring. Neither was the group helped by the lay-off they suffered during 1980-81, as this latest line-up shattered and October was left, again, to pick up the pieces alone. Despite releasing a string of generally fine 45's, Chelsea's public profile had slipped below the bread line. Press notices weren't only few and far between, they were also impatient. "Don't say the buggers are still at it!"

EVACUATE, the combo's second all-new album, was recorded with an entirely new line-up — several, in fact, as the membership continued shifting even as Chelsea motored on through 1981-82. Indeed, the band took on the quality of a revolving door — no sooner did fans get used to one line-up, than there was another to take its place, and when continuity left the group, so, unfortunately, did any sense of lasting quality.

When they were good, though, they were incredibly powerful, as the 1999 reunion of the CHELSEA era line-up proved. Triumphant across the course of that year's Social Chaos tour of America, backed up by a string of reissues supervised by Stevenson's own Pink Gun label, Chelsea proved, once again, that there were few groups who could top them. And even fewer performers with more magnetic dynamism than Gene October.

CHELSEA DISCOGRAPHY
UK Singles
- *Right to Work / The Loner* (Step Forward SF2, 1977)
- *High Rise Living / No Admission* (Step Forward SF5, 1977)
- *Urban Kids / No Flowers* (Step Forward SF8, 1978)
- *No-one's Coming / What Would You Do?* (Step Forward SF14, 1980)
- *Look At The Outside / Don't Get Me Wrong* (Step Forward SF15, 1980)
- *No Escape / Decide* (Step Forward SF16, 1980)
- *Rocking House / Years Away* (Step Forward SF17, 1981)
- *Freemans / ID Parade / How Do You Know* (Step Forward SF18, 1981)
- *Evacuate / New Era* (Step Forward SF20, 1981)
- *War Across The Nation /* (Step Forward SF21, 1982)
- *Stand Out / Last Drink* (Step Forward SF22, 1982)

US Single
- *I'm On Fire / ?* (IRS IR 9004, 1978)

UK Albums
- CHELSEA (Step Forward SFLP2, 1979)
- ALTERNATIVE HITS (Step Forward SFLP5, 1981)
- EVACUATE (Step Forward SFLP7, 1982)
- JUST FOR THE RECORD (Step Forward SFLP 10, 1984)
- LIVE AT THE MUSIC MACHINE 1978 (Released Emotions REM 016, 1992)
- UNRELEASED STUFF (1978 out-takes) (Clay CLAY 101, 1988)
- CHELSEA (Captain Oi AHOY CD91, 1999)
- ALTERNATIVE HITS (Captain Oi AHOYCD 92, 1999)
- EVACUATE (Captain Oi AHOYCD 94, 1999)
- THE PUNK SINGLES COLLECTION (Captain Oi AHOYCD 98, 1999)
- PUNK ROCK RARITIES (Captain Oi AHOYCD 106, 1999)

⋘ 11 ⋙
Eater

EATER! They were no more than schoolboys, but they were one of the first bands to see where the Pistols were taking things, and when you caught them live you could almost think they were going places. Of course they weren't, but over the course of their first two singles at least, they tried. Bloody hard!

Formed in Finchley, north London, Eater took their name from a Marc Bolan lyric, a line in the song *Suneye*. The original line-up — which did no more than talk of its dreams for the future — included future Otway-Barrett protege Eddie Stanton. By the time of the group's first gig, at their school in November 1976, however, they had settled down to Andy Blade (vocals), Brian Chevette (guitar), Ian Woodcock (bass) and Phil "Social Demise" Rowland (drums.)

Rowland quit; he was replaced by 14 year old Rodger "Dee Generate" Bullen, introduced to the group by The Damned's Rat Scabies. Apparently, the youngster had not been able to get enough time out of class to rehearse for the first show. He was on board, however, for Eater's "official" debut, booking a hall in Manchester, sharing the bill with The Buzzcocks and armed with stolen guitars. Their entire repertoire, Blade continues, comprised "speeded up versions of old Velvets songs."

That band's *Sweet Jane*, at least, would remain in Eater's set. Elsewhere, combining surprisingly savage punk originals — *Outside View*, *Bedroom Fix* and the like — with a startlingly fresh interpretation of Alice Cooper's *I'm Eighteen* (revalued to become *I'm 15*), Eater swiftly found their way into a lot of hearts when they announced in their first interview that Johnny Rotten was "too old." The grand old man of punk, after all, was already approaching his 22nd birthday.

Eater's own tender years, however, did not always work in their favor. In early December, a show at the Hope & Anchor was interrupted when the police swooped in, investigating allegations of child labor violations. Only the intercession of the band members' parents prevented Eater being added to the already lengthening list of punk rock martyrs — just

days, after all, had passed since The Sex Pistols' infamous TODAY show appearance and all over the country the authorities were girding their loins to repel punk boarders.

Signing to The Label, Eater's first single, *Outside View*, was a deliriously gratuitous slice of punk trash and, caught in concert for the LIVE AT THE ROXY album, the group hammered into place two of the most competent performances in sight, *I'm 15* and their own *Don't Need It.* They celebrated the coup by rushing out what was to become their best ever single before the Roxy album was even off the presses.

Thinking Of The USA arrived in June and won the group all manner of accolades, and though they spent much of the remaining year gigging, they still found time to record their debut album, THE ALBUM, for release in January 1978. Previewed by a new single, *Lock It Up*, the album was a storming triumph, the band's original punkish abrasiveness giving way only slightly to a petulant power pop sheen, one which was amplified even further by the live-at-Dingwalls GET YOUR YO-YOS OUT EP.

Growth, however, did not necessarily equate with harmony. Dee Generate quit over "musical differences," and with Phil Rowland back in the drum seat, Eater lurched into 1978 with much of their initial enthusiasm and excitement already far in the past. When the delightful *What She Wants She Needs* power pop anthem collapsed, Eater weren't too far behind it. They split in January 1979.

EATER DISCOGRAPHY
UK Singles
- *Outside View / You* (The Label TLR 001, 1977)
- *Thinking Of The USA / Space Dreaming* (The Label TLR 003, 1977)
- *Lock It Up / Jeepster* (The Label TLR 004, 1977)
- GET YOUR YOYOS OUT EP (The Label TLR 007, 1978)
- *What She Wants She Needs / Reaching For The Sky* (The Label TLR 009, 1978)

UK Albums
- THE ALBUM (The Label LP 001, 1978)

Important UK Archive Releases
- LIVE AT THE ROXY, WC2 (compilation including *I Don't Need It*) (Receiver RR132, 1991)
- THE COMPLEAT EATER (compilation) (Anagram PUNK 10, 1993)

≪ 12 ≫
Generation X

Billy Idol was never your average neighborhood punk. Even during the summer of 1977 he stood out, screaming the odds from behind a jailbait mask of glitter and glamor which had more in common with a Hollywood starlet than anything so sordid as a Punk Rocker.

Like Johnny Rotten, Joe Strummer and Brian James, Idol had looked around at the state of music and found it wanting. Unlike them, however, he did not want to destroy, he wanted to beautify. He did not revile the superstars of yesterday, he parodied them — even his adopted surname was a subtle jab at the manufactured marvels whose stranglehold punk had come to shatter. "Punk has always been about getting up and doing something for yourself," Idol reminded his detractors in 1983. "And that is exactly what I'm doing."

The original Generation X exploded out of the wreckage of Gene October's first Chelsea line-up. Leaving the group name alone with the vocalist, and with Idol taking over the microphone, the group — Idol, bassist Tony James and drummer John Towe, plus newly recruited guitarist Bob Andrews — named themselves for a Swinging London paperback, then set about recreating that same era's image for their own.

Debuting at London's Central College of Art and Design on December 12, 1976, Generation X would then become the first band ever to play the Roxy, both during its trial run in December and following its full-time opening on January 15. Much to the group's own astonishment, by the time they graduated from that particular academy they were ranked among the hottest unsigned groups around. Yet Idol insisted it had all started off as a joke.

Generation X

"It grew out of the fact that we were bored, and when I first started with Generation X, it was because punk was so extremely unpopular. We were the absolute antithesis of Led Zeppelin and Foreigner and Journey, and the funny thing is, we didn't even think there was any money in it. It was a massive joke to us when we were playing the Roxy, and there were all these record company people giving us their cards. We didn't give a damn, but these people wanted us so much we could pick and choose."

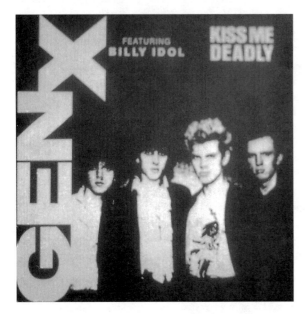

Towe quit to be replaced by Mark Laff, stolen away from Subway Sect, and Generation X signed to Chrysalis that spring, celebrating with a "coming out" show at the Marquee, opened by the newly emergent Lurkers. Their debut single, *Your Generation*, followed — a great teenaged anthem which lost no time in driving straight into the British Top 40. It was followed in November by *Wild Youth*, an even better song but one, inexplicably, which flopped dramatically. All was put to rights in the new year, however, when first, *Ready Steady Go* reached No. 47, and then when the group's self-named debut album appeared.

The album was recorded with producer Martin Rushent, and Idol's latter-day misgivings about the sound of the record are best viewed in the light of Rushent's own schedule of the time. "He was trying to mix us, mix The Stranglers, run the United Artists A&R department and do 999 all at the same time." Neither did it help that the entire album was recorded in just seven days, inside a studio James later described as "a shithole."

One of the group's ideas around this time was to record a dub version of the set, to be called GENERATION Z. But despite James' belief that "if I keep pestering the record company long enough they'll let us do it," the record never happened. "You're not a reggae band," Chrysalis would say whenever the subject came up . . . In the end, only one track — *Wild Dub* — made it out, as the flip side of *Wild Youth*.

Another dubious production decision saw Generation X spend the summer of 1978 recording their second album with Ian Hunter, of Mott The Hoople fame. It was an odd combination — an idol of the early-mid 70's glam explosion in cahoots with idols of the decade-end's punk movement — and VALLEY OF THE DOLLS, the result of these sessions, was suitably schizophrenic. But *King Rocker*, a tribute to Elvis Presley, was to become the biggest hit of the band's career, and it really didn't seem to matter what the UK music press thought of Generation X.

King Rocker reached No. 11, but the album all but bombed, peaking at a miserly No. 51, a failing which the group members themselves countered by expressing their own dissatisfaction with the record. "It was a disgusting display of a group who didn't understand why they were a group," Idol later complained. "Ian Hunter did his best, but he didn't know what the group was about."

Neither, it seemed, did Generation X. Further singles — the title track and *Friday's Angels* — both illustrated just how out of touch with current tastes the band had drifted, Hollywood sleaze epics which had no common ground whatsoever with the bitter landscapes of 1978-79. Management problems rose to the fore ("they were becoming rich and we weren't," James remarked) and, as the band foundered, its musical direction became a battleground.

copyright 1984 Phil Anderson / KAOS2000 Magazine

While Laff and Andrews battled to preserve the band's raucous roots, Idol and James pushed ahead with their visions of a dance rock sound modeled on the chic club sounds of New York and Tokyo. Finally, Idol issued an ultimatum — "I sat down and told them if they didn't do this *Dancing With Myself / White Wedding* music, I was going to leave the group." Instead, the dissenters quit.

A new line-up quickly came together, Idol and James joined by former Clash drummer Terry Chimes and guitarist James Stevenson from a later incarnation of Chelsea. Steve New (The Rich Kids), Danny Kustow (Tom Robinson Band), Steve Jones (Sex Pistols) and John McGeogh (Magazine) would also grace the studio as the group worked on their third album, only for Chrysalis to come within an ace of not even releasing it.

"They didn't want it out because they thought it wouldn't sell," Idol scolded. "They didn't see the purpose in pushing a record that wasn't going to be a big one, or one by a group that was going to split up." In the end, KISS ME DEADLY (released under the abbreviated name of Gen X) shifted some 50,000 copies, most of them posthumously.

A British tour in December 1980 made it obvious to all that the band was on its last legs. "We just weren't giving the fans what they deserved," Idol admitted. The group's final single was *Dancing With Myself*, their first ever 12". It reached the Top 70 and stopped dead, but critical reaction was so good that in the new year, Chrysalis — obviously taken by surprise — remixed it for a prompt reissue. This time, it hit No. 60.

Too little, too late. In January, 1981, Idol moved to New York to work with new manager Bill Aucoin and producer Keith Forsey on a reworked version of *Dancing With Myself*. A solo star was born. James formed the brilliant Sigue Sigue Sputnik. It was 1993 before he and Idol worked together again, when they crowned the singer's latest London show with a half hour Generation X reunion.

GENERATION X DISCOGRAPHY
UK Singles
- *Your Generation / Day By Day* (Chrysalis CHS 2165, 1977)
- *Wild Youth / No No No* [mispressing] (Chrysalis CHS 2189, 1977)
- *Wild Youth / Wild Dub* (Chrysalis CHS 2189, 1977)
- *Ready Steady Go /* (Chrysalis CHS 2207, 1978)
- *King Rocker / Gimme Some Truth* (Chrysalis CHS 2261, 1978)
- *Valley Of The Dolls / Shakin' All Over* (Chrysalis CHS 2310, 1979)
- *Friday's Angels / Trying For Kicks / This Heat* (Chrysalis CHS 2330, 1979)
- *Dancing With Myself / Ugly Rash* (Chrysalis CHS 2444, 1980)
- *Dancing With Myself / Ugly Rash / Loopy Dub* (12") (Chrysalis CHS 122444, 1980)
- *Dancing With Myself / Untouchables / King Rocker* (Chrysalis CHS 2488, 1981)
- *Dancing With Myself / Untouchables / King Rocker / Rock On* (12") (Chrysalis CHS 122488, 1981)

UK Albums
- GENERATION X (Chrysalis CHR 1169, 1978)
- VALLEY OF THE DOLLS (Chrysalis CHR 193, 1979)
- KISS ME DEADLY (Chrysalis CHR 1327, 1981)
- THE BEST OF (Chrysalis CHM 1521, 1985)
- THE ORIGINAL GENERATION X (MBC JOCKLP 9, 1987)
- GENERATION X LIVE (MBC JOCKLP 11, 1988)
- PERFECT HITS (Chrysalis 1854, 1991)

≺ 13 ≻
The Lurkers

One of the longest survived sagas in the entire annals of punk, The Lurkers started life in Uxbridge, west London, in late 1976, unabashedly as indebted to The Ramones as the Pistols, but boasting a mock-Cockney swagger which was utterly unique. Rehearsing in a basement beneath the Fulham-based Beggars Banquet record store, it was The Lurkers' search for management that would launch the Beggars record label dynasty — founders

Nick Austin and Martin Mills were already running a tour promotion company. Failing to find a record label interested in taking The Lurkers, the duo decided to start their own and, in July 1977, the band's debut single, *Shadow*, was produced for free distribution at live shows.

The group previewed the single with their highest profile gig yet, opening for Generation X at the Marquee, at a show celebrating the headliners' recent recruitment to Chrysalis.

The original line-up of Howard Wall (vocals), Pete Stride (guitar), Arturo Bassick (bass) and Manic Esso (drums) broke apart soon after, when Bassick quit. He was replaced by former Saints mainstay Kym Bradshaw and The Lurkers unleashed *Freak Show* that fall. Bradshaw was then replaced by Nigel Moore and, the following spring, The Lurkers finally scored the hit single that their escalating live support demanded, the impressive *Ain't Got A Clue*.

The Lurkers' debut album, FULHAM FALLOUT followed, launching the band onto a streak of almost unbelievably fine 45's — *I Don't Need To Tell Her* and *Just Thirteen* led up to the release of the sophomore album GOD'S LONELY MEN. The *Out In The Dark* and *New Guitar In Town* singles followed, the latter showcasing The Lurkers' newest member, ex-Boys guitarist John Plain. In this form, work immediately began on new material, previewed in November by a four song session recorded for the JOHN PEEL Show.

Recorded, but never broadcast. Seemingly without any warning whatsoever, the unthinkable happened — the group broke up. The fate of the second album had a lot to do with it, a strong set which was savaged by the press and ignored by the public. Neither of the group's most recent singles climbed above No. 72 on the chart; when Pete Stride and John Plain, himself still smarting from The Boys' own continued lack of success, began work on an album of their own, titled after the last Lurkers' 45, the writing was clearly on the wall. (Fittingly, Lurkers vocalist Wall would subsequently join The Boys, in time for their final single and an Italian tour.)

Of course, the breach wasn't permanent. The Lurkers reunited around Stride, Moore and Esso (now working under his given name, Pete Haynes) in 1982 and, though another break-up followed two years later, in 1988 Bassick rejoined the core trio and The Lurkers lurked again.

LURKERS DISCOGRAPHY

Singles

- *Shadow* (free with show admission) / *Love Story* (Beggars Banquet BEG 1, 1977)
- *Freak Show* / *Mass Media Believer* (Beggars Banquet BEG 2, 1977)
- *Ain't Got A Clue* / *Ooh Ooh I Love You* (Beggars Banquet BEG 6, 1978)
- *Chaos Bros Fulham Fallout Firty-Free* (flexi) (Beggars Banquet BEG 6 192, 1978)
- *I Don't Need To Tell Her* / *Pills* / (Beggars Banquet BEG 9, 1978)
- *Just Thirteen* / *Countdown* (Beggars Banquet BEG 14, 1979)
- OUT IN THE DARK EP: *Cyanide* / *Suzie Is A Floozie* / *Cyanide* (pub version) (Beggars Banquet BEG 19, 1979)
- *Shadow* / *Love Story* / *Freak Show* / *Mass Media Believer* (doublepack single) (Beggars Banquet BACK 1, 1979)
- *I Don't Need To Tell Her* / *Pills* / *Just Thirteen* / *Countdown* (doublepack single) (Beggars Banquet BACK 3, 1979)
- *New Guitar In Town* / *Little Ol' Wine Drinker Me* (Beggars Banquet BEG 28, 1979)

Albums

- FULHAM FALLOUT (Beggars Banquet BEGA 2, 1978)
- GOD'S LONELY MEN (Beggars Banquet BEGA 8, 1979)
- LAST WILL & TESTAMENT (compilation) (Beggars Banquet BOPA 2, 1980)
- THE BBC PUNK SESSIONS (Captain Oi! AHOY 137, 2000)

≪ 14 ≫
Johnny Moped

In any discussion of punk's greatest legends, the name of Johnny Moped forever looms large — not necessarily for the vitality of their vinyl, although few would deny that the Moped had few peers in that arena. Nor through the brilliant chaos of their live shows, although once again, a good Moped gig could keep you grinning for a week. No, Johnny Moped was a legend because with a reputation and a presentation like theirs, what else could they be?

Johnny Moped, the man and the band (they were not mutually exclusive), did not materialize out of nowhere. Early stirrings featuring Dave Berk (drums), Maxim Trash, singer Xerxes and Ray Burns, who handled guitar, bass and keyboards, were captured on the group's *Disco Girls* single, taped in 1975 but unreleased till 1979. Moped's own musical apprenticeship came in Johnny Moped & The Five Arrogant Superstars, an outfit comprising himself, Xerxes, Berk, Burns, guitarist Fred Gunge and keyboard player Phil Burns.

The Johnny Moped Band itself, however, formed around mid-76, lining up as Johnny (vocals), Ray Burns (guitar), and the Dave and Fred Berk rhythm section. Burns, of course, was not long for that world, changing his name to Captain Sensible and heading off to play bass with The Damned. He made amends, however, by introducing his own chosen successor, Slimey Toad — once a compatriot of Rat Scabies in Rot, an arty disaster whose greatest achievement was a residency at St Laurence's Mental Home.

Early recruits to the Roxy roster, Johnny Moped were caught in fine, if undisciplined, form on the LIVE AT THE ROXY album, hammering out *Hard Lovin' Man*. The sound of that song was the sound of archetypal Moped, heavy R&B slobbering through a meat grinder and hung out for the fire ants. It sounded incompetent, but the best Moped gigs always did, a fumbling, bumbling, grumbling noise which boasted all the proficiency of a blind man playing poker. The Chiswick label, however, was more than impressed and towards the end of 1977, Moped's debut single, *No-One*, hit the streets.

An album, CYCLEDELIC, followed in May, 1978, promptly taking the alternative charts by storm, while the bizarre (but characteristically so) *Darling, Let's Have Another Baby* single remains something of an underground classic to this day — erstwhile Chiswick label-mates Kirsty MacColl (ex-Drug Addix) and Billy Bragg (ex-Riff Raff) teamed up for a version when they guested on John Peel's radio show together. The late Mick Ronson was also known to throw it into his live set on occasion.

Constant calls for a less shambolic rendition of *Hard Lovin' Man* prompted the group to take a second live version, from a Roundhouse show in February 1978, for release on the flip of their third single, Chuck Berry's *Little Queenie*. It was phenomenal, all the more so since a guest appearance from Ray Burns finally gave the world a chance to hear what the original Moped was occasionally capable of. And of course, it was utterly appropriate that Johnny Moped's first recorded song should also become their last. The group broke up shortly after *Little Queenie* hit the streets.

Although a number of abortive sessions were rumored over the next decade or so, Moped himself remained in self-imposed obscurity, his only confirmed resurfacing being the Toad-Berk composed *Save The Baby Seals* session, originally intended for release on a 1983 Artists For Animals compilation. The silence was broken again in the early 1990's by the all-new SEARCH FOR XERXES album, only to be restored immediately after. Close to another decade has passed since then, and Moped remains a mystery.

Which is probably just as well. Nothing kills a legend as fast as visibility.

JOHNNY MOPED DISCOGRAPHY

UK Singles

- ○ *No-one / Incendiary Device* (Chiswick S15, 1977)
- ○ *Darling, Let's Have Another Baby / Something Else / It Really Digs* (Chiswick NS27, 1978)
- ○ *Little Queenie / Hard Lovin' Man* (Chiswick NS41, 1978)
- ○ *Basically The Original J Moped Tape / cont* (Chiswick PROMO 3, 1978)

UK Albums

- ○ LIVE AT THE ROXY WC2 (compilation including *Hard Lovin' Man* (Harvest SHSP 4069, 1977)
- ○ CYCLEDELIC (Chiswick WIK 8, 1978)

⋖ 15 ⋗
Penetration

Pauline Murray (vocals), Robert Blamire (bass), Gary Smallman (drums) and Gary Chapman (guitar) were bored teenagers rattling around the northern mining community of Ferrybridge when they formed Penetration — the nearest cities, Newcastle and Middlesbrough, already had formative punk scenes and, of course, all four had traveled down to Manchester when The Sex Pistols played there.

But still, it was astonishing how quickly Penetration (named for a track on the Stooges' RAW POWER album) took off. One week they were playing the Middlesbrough Rock Garden, wowing the weirdies with a tight, melodic set which found a middle ground between Patti Smith and The Buzzcocks, and the next they were invited to open for Generation X at the Roxy in London after a copy of their first demo tape reached that band's ears.

Over the next few months, Penetration commuted regularly between the capital and Newcastle, growing increasingly impressive every time they played. Murray herself was spellbinding, a black-clad oasis of control and calm within the most chaotic surroundings, her alternately sweet and strident vocals instinctively counterpointing the band's own energies. The best of their set — *Don't Dictate, Moving Targets,* Patti Smith's *Free Money* — told you everything you needed to know about Penetration — which was, they weren't going to remain unsigned and unknown for long.

In March, 1977, the group handed a copy of their latest demo to the manager of the Newcastle branch of the Virgin record store chain. He passed it on to the company's London-based record label and, that summer, Virgin signed Penetration to a one-off single deal. Unsurprisingly, their debut was *Don't Dictate* and, though it didn't chart, it did encourage Virgin to give Penetration a full deal.

Guitarist Chaplin quit to form his own group, Soul On Ice, to be replaced by Neale Floyd in time for Penetration's second single, *Firing Squad*, in May 1978. A second guitarist, Fred Purser followed in July and, in October, Penetration finally released their debut album, the gargantuan MOVING TARGETS. It made No. 22 on the UK chart, as the band toured ferociously. However, their twin guitar assault had added a discomforting element to the Penetration sound.

No matter the ambition of their earlier songs, the execution ensured an edgy factiousness which derailed any notions of pomp and circumstance before they got started. Now, Penetration screamed out in full hi-fi splendour — *Danger Signs*, in April 1979, was a great single but, as the punk / new wave ranks began to close against the intrusion of anything that didn't belt along at 100 mph, it was a great Rock single. Which in turn meant that Penetration were a great Rock combo, and their audience began to shift restlessly.

Work on Penetration's sophomore album, COMING UP FOR AIR, continued apace, but the group members themselves seemed to be losing interest in all things punk and new wave shaped. Titles like *She Is The Slave*, *Killed In The Rush* and *Shout Above The Noise* didn't help their cause either — elsewhere in northern England, the first stirrings of what would become the New Wave Of British Heavy Metal were making themselves felt in the same clubs that punk had first taken root, and that increasingly seemed the direction in which Penetration appeared to be heading.

Reviews were uniformly disparaging, gigs were simply depressing. Finally, in October, Murray announced the band was splitting. "I never wanted to be in Penetration and to be worrying all the time. I wanted it

Penetration

to be fun, not to be always thinking of hit singles and cracking America and writing for the next LP." The group's official farewell show at Newcastle City Hall was recorded for future reference, and a handful of contractual obligation gigs over the next couple of weeks offered nothing to change the band's minds.

The members' subsequent activities were, to put it bluntly, inevitable. While Murray and Blamire remained together, linking with producer Martin Hannett and ex-Buzzcock John Maher at the soul of the ad hoc Invisible Girls, Purser indeed led the charge into what could have been Penetration's own destiny, forming relentless metal masters Tygers Of Pang Tang.

PENETRATION DISCOGRAPHY
Singles
- ○ *Don't Dictate / Money Talks* (Virgin VS 192, 1977)
- ○ *Firing Squad / Never* (Virgin VS 213, 1978)
- ○ *Life's A Gamble / VIP* (Virgin VS 226, 1978)
- ○ *Danger Signs / Stone Heroes* (Virgin VS 257, 1979)
- ○ *Danger Sings / Stone Heroes / Version* (12") (Virgin VS 25712, 1979)
- ○ *Come Into The Open / Lifeline* (Virgin VS 268, 1979)

Albums
- ○ MOVING TARGETS (Virgin V2109, 1978)
- ○ COMING UP FOR AIR (Virgin V2131, 1979)
- ○ BBC RADIO ONE IN CONCERT (1979) (Windsong WIN 009, 1991)
- ○ PENETRATION (demos / live compilation) (Burning Airlines PILOT 1, 1993)

◄ 16 ►
Sham 69

"Hersham boys, Hersham boys, lace up boots and corduroys." Jimmy Pursey was never the most fashion conscious gent around. But when Sham 69 first shrugged off the Bay City Roller tendencies which kept their first pre-punk stirrings as obscure as you could wish, and embraced instead the punk rock music that had finally filtered through to Pursey's stock broker belt home of, indeed, Hersham, their earliest supporters couldn't give a toss what they wore.

Neither could Sham. They didn't care about the niceties of the music business, either. Probably they didn't know there even was such a thing. Instead, they blasted into the public consciousness with an almost naive faith in the tenets of punk and a touching belief that simply saying something with sincerity was enough to make people listen.

"The rest of the band were like me, local mates playing up a dead end," Pursey explained. "They were terrible before I joined. Hadn't a clue what was going on." Taking their name from the remains of some graffiti on a toilet wall at the local soccer club ("Hersham 69" referred to some long forgotten glory), Pursey, bassist Albie Slider, guitarists Neil Harris and Johnny Goodfornothing, and Billy Bostik (drums) began playing low key London shows around the end of 1976, slowly inching up the circuit to the Roxy as 1977 got underway.

Still they were little more than a whisper in June, when Pursey decided it was time to begin putting his own dreams into action. Goodfornothing, Harris and Bostik were fired. In their stead came guitarist Dave Parsons (who swiftly emerged as Pursey's songwriting partner) and drummer Mark Cain, just as Sham was approached to cut a one-off single for Sniffin' Glue impresario Mark P's Step Forward label.

Produced by former Velvet Underground bassist John Cale, then in London to check out the punk scene for himself, *I Don't Wanna* was gore-grizzled proto-punk, all chorus and balls and certainly sufficiently crude to fuel the growing comparisons with glam era pop stompers Slade which were now springing up everywhere. True, Sham could spell things better, but elsewhere . . . The crucial difference was, while Slade had started their career flirting with the skinheads, then got out as quickly as they could, Sham looked like letting the little spiky-tops take the whole thing over.

Slider left the group in October 1977, just as the single came out. In his place came Dave Treganna and Sham got their best break yet when, taking advantage of the suspicion swirling around the opening of a new "specialist" punk club in London's Wardour Street, the Vortex, Pursey announced Sham would play an alternative show on a neighboring rooftop. It was all very GET BACK, of course, and Pursey ended up getting arrested for his pains. But the thirty pound fine was probably the best money he'd ever spent — the ensuing press coverage was beyond his wildest dreams.

Signing to Polydor at the end of the year, Sham's next single, *Borstal Breakout*, was unveiled in January 1978, establishing the mold from which Sham was never truly to escape. Pounding, stamping, drums-like-feet, roaring guitars, a mindless chant and Pursey's purpose-built Cockney shout-sing. "People say I've got a big mouth," Pursey mused years later. "Well maybe I have, but we haven't changed, we're just like we were when we played the Roxy. That's why I admire people like The Clash and The Jam, and why I despise Siouxsie & the Banshees, cos she's now trying to say she was never a punk, when she used to flash her tits around the 100 Club. We're just ordinary, and it's not hip to be ordinary any more. That's why we're not big stars and we don't want to be. But we're with the kids and that's the most important thing."

Ah, the kids . . . With the single fuelling Sham's growing exposure, the demand to see them grew — along with the media's insistence that every review of the band also threw in a mention of their skinhead following. It was inevitable, under those circumstances, that the neo-Nazi National Front should cotton onto the group as well, seeing in the vast shaven-headed Sham Army a way of bringing their own message to the pop kid masses — regardless of how Sham themselves felt about it.

In fact, the band desperately tried to distance themselves from the foul rhetoric which the Front delightedly heaped onto their shoulders, but once the shit hit, it stuck — all the more so after Pursey, warming to the notion that he was a Leader Of Men of sorts, announced, "the kids can relate to me because I used to smash windows, beat up Pakis and things like that." He really didn't mean it to come out like it sounded. But of course, it did.

The growing clouds of controversy could not overshadow Sham's commercial ascent. *Angels With Dirty Faces*, their latest single, made the Top 20 (No. 19.) the studio / live TELL US THE TRUTH album scraped the Top 30. And, in the summer of 1978, that most eternal of itinerant soccer chants, *If The Kids Are United* was slamming the group into the Top 10. Three months later the infuriatingly unforgettable *Hurry Up Harry* was to follow it there. And all over the country, the Sham army had a new refrain to contemplate — "We're going down the pub." As if they'd ever gone anywhere else.

What next? A concept album, naturally. "It's gonna be kinda like QUADROPHENIA, that album done by the Who," Pursey elucidated. "One song will be in a cafe with pinballs and so on, then a railway station, all sorts of places. It'll be like a concept, but it's things that mean something to people, about situations they can understand."

It already sounded tremendously exciting, but Pursey was barely warmed up yet. "I was gonna call it A DAY IN THE LIFE OF JOE BLOGGS, because that's what it's about. It's essentially about one person, but it refers to almost everyone in this country. What I want to make sure is that every song relates to certain individuals. It's what Sham 69's about, relating songs to different people."

Patronizing or precious? How much of Sham was a sham? Certainly the band had the energy and the commitment to stand up for everything they spoke of. Indeed, despite (or, just as likely, because of) the continued efforts of the National Front to rally Sham's following to their own hateful cause, Pursey became a fiercely outspoken supporter of Rock Against Racism, even making two highly publicized (and well-received) solo appearances at RAR showcases, with The Clash at Victoria Park in 1978, and with a Jake Burns (Stiff Little Fingers) and Tony James (Generation X) fired pickup group at Alexandra Palace in 1979.

It's true, too, that Sham songs worked precisely because they were about the common herd, and dealt with themes which the common herd understood. They hovered in the gray area between working class and the unemployed, popping holes in the belly of the social structure and trying to prove to the world that not everyone who liked a bit of rough'n'tumble was a bike-chain toting retard who'd spent his last half a braincell on a pair of Doc Martens.

But the headlines that were snowballing around Sham insisted otherwise. Fights at their shows were commonplace, and riots only a little less so. In Sham, one critic mused, we were witnessing the final decline of man and, in their audience, the bottle hurling, racist cracking, fist flying death machine which lumbered out whenever the group hit town, we witnessed the fate that awaited after the decline. The band themselves were helpless to intercede — Pursey was regularly reduced to tears, begging the fighting to stop, but it never did and the next night, he'd be up onstage doing it all again.

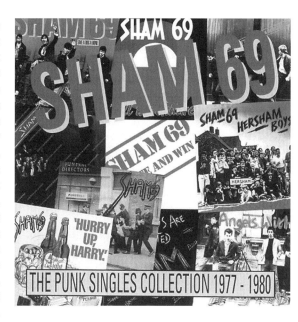

Something had to give and, at Middlesex Polytechnic in January 1979, it did. As a BBC camera crew filmed Sham's performance for the arts show ARENA, the zooplankton on-lookers denigrated into violence, wrecking the concert hall in the process. And two nights later in Aylesbury, Pursey finally attained martyrdom. This is it, the last gig we'll ever play.

The last gig, maybe. But Sham weren't really dead. March 1979 brought *Questions And Answers*, August gave us *Hersham Boys* and, though it still represents one of the lyrical nadirs of the entire new wave, an outlandish paean to the fighting togs adopted by ... the local skins? But Jimmy, we thought you weren't talking to those guys anymore! — regardless it was to become Sham's biggest hit ever.

Again, the final curtain was rung down. Sham split up in June 1979, then returned in July to promote their third album, THE ADVENTURES OF THE HERSHAM BOYS. They followed up with tours of the UK and the US — whose immigration earthworms, obviously stung by the vicious *No Entry* a year earlier ("they won't let us in the USA, we didn't want to go there anyway"), had finally lifted a ban on the artists. The album hit the Top 10. But even in their hour of reborn triumph, Sham remained shaky.

From being a media darling, Pursey's increasingly tazaddikim affirmation of his own worth had finally worn out its welcome. Similarly, while his generally appropriate protestations of victimization had always found a ready public ear in the past, his own constant habit of recanting even the most sincere sounding gesture (group break-ups a case in point) now made everything he uttered sound hollow and false. From the top of the world in early 1979, Sham 69 would spend 1980 experiencing life at the other end of the spectrum altogether.

A positively appalling cover of The Yardbirds' *You're A Better Man Than I* barely made the Top 50. Another single, *Tell The Children* scarcely improved on that and *Unite And Win* didn't even make the chart. Sham was turned down for a role in the Who's QUADROPHENIA movie and finally, their new album, THE GAME, bombed completely. The band broke up once again — and this time there'd be no going back. Pursey announced a solo career. His colleagues teamed up with the Dead Boys' Stiv Bators in The Wanderers.

The solo career faltered swiftly. Finding himself a pariah in his homeland (many venues, reacting to the violence which had so tarnished Sham's name, refused to even book him), Pursey turned instead towards the one outlet where he could be taken seriously, producing the Angelic Upstarts and the Cockney Rejects, two of the groups most obviously harnessed to Sham's star. But that too, faltered after a handful of releases, and Pursey spent much of the 1980's adrift.

It was inevitable, then, that a reunion with Parsons in 1987 would lead swiftly to a return to Sham 69 and so it proved. Gigging furiously, recording sporadically, Sham 69 finally proved the truth behind at least one of their greatest hits. Apparently, they could never be divided, either.

SHAM 69 DISCOGRAPHY
UK Singles
- *I Don't Wanna* / *Ulster* / *Red London* (Step Forward SF 4, 1977)
- *What Have We Got?* (one sided flexi) (no label, 1978)
- *Borstal Breakout* / *Hey, Little Rich Boy* (Polydor 2058 966, 1978)
- *Song Of The Streets* (one sided flexi) (no label, 1978)
- *Angels With Dirty Faces* / *Cockney Kids . . .* (Polydor 2059 023, 1978)
- *Kids Are United* / *Sunday Morning Nightmare* (Polydor 2059 050, 1978)
- *Hurry Up Harry* / *No Entry* (Polydor 2059 065, 1978)

- *Questions & Answers / I Gotta Survive / Little Help From My Friends* (Polydor POSP 27, 1979)
- *Hersham Boys / Tell Us The Truth / I Don't Wanna* (Polydor POSP 64, 1979)
- *Hersham Boys / Tell Us The Truth / Rip Off / I'm A Man / I Don't Wanna* (12") (Polydor POSPX 64, 1979)
- *Borstal Breakout / If The Kids Are United 1979* (12" free with LP ADVENTURES) (Polydor 2812 045, 1979)
- *You're A Better Man / Give The Dog A Bone* (Polydor POSP 82, 1979)
- *Tell The Children / Jack* (Polydor POSP 136, 1980)
- *Unite And Win / I'm A Man* (Polydor 2059 259, 1980)
- *Voices / Money / Who Gives A Damn / That's Life* (Polydor 2816 028, 1980)
- *Angels With Dirty Faces / Borstal Breakout / Hurry Up Harry / Kids Are United* (Polydor POSPX 602, 1982)
- LIVE EP: *Borstal Breakout / Kids Are United / Angels With Dirty Faces / Rip Off* (Receiver 3016, 1991)

UK Albums
- TELL US THE TRUTH (Polydor 2383 491, 1978)
- THAT'S LIFE (Polydor POLD 5010, 1978)
- ADVENTURES OF THE HERSHAM BOYS (Polydor POLD 5025, 1979)
- THE GAME (Polydor POLD 5033, 1980)
- THE FIRST, THE BEST, THE LIVE (Polydor 2383 596, 1980)
- ANGELS WITH DIRTY FACES (Receiver RRLP 104, 1986)
- LIVE AND LOUD! (Link LP 04, 1987)
- LIVE AND LOUD VOLUME 2 (Link LP 025, 1988)
- SHAM'S LAST STAND LIVE (Link MLP 075, 1989)
- THE BEST AND THE REST OF ... Live (Receiver RRLP 112, 1989)
- THE COMPLETE LIVE (compilation) (Castle CLALP 153, 1989)
- LIVE AT THE ROXY (Receiver RRLP 133, 1990)
- BBC RADIO ONE IN CONCERT (1979) (Windsong WIN 049, 1993)
- RARITIES 1977-80 (Captain Oi! AHOY 139, 2000)

≺ 17 ≻
Slaughter And The Dogs

Armed with a pristine white Les Paul he'd been given by Mick Ronson, 16 year old Mick Rossi formed Slaughter And The Dogs in April 1976 with three fellow Wythenshawe, Manchester, school kids — green-haired vocalist Wayne Barrett, bassist Howard Bates and drummer Mad Muffet.

The band took its name from a combination of Ronson's first post-Bowie album, SLAUGHTER ON 10TH AVENUE and Bowie's first post-Ronson release, DIAMOND DOGS.

Musically, however, their inspirations were the local example of The Buzzocks and the visiting magic of The Sex Pistols and, thus equipped, Slaughter would throw themselves first into the local scene, then onto London. They appeared on the original LIVE AT THE ROXY album, introducing themselves as Murder And The Cats and emerging two songs (*Runaways* and *Boston Babies*) later among the stars of the show, a billing which their debut single, *Cranked Up Really High*, effortlessly reinforced.

Their first release for the Manchester label Rabid, *Cranked Up* was a punk chart hit that spring, paving the way for Slaughter to sign with Decca (the last of the major labels to jump aboard the punk bandwagon) and follow through that fall with another deathless anthem, *Where Have All The Boot Boys Gone?* (they're probably all at Sham gigs, was the inevitable response.)

Dame To Blame followed, as the group got to work on their debut album, a set which would be further dignified by a guest appearance from Ronson. DO IT DOG STYLE emerged a masterpiece. Slaughter played with a rare conviction and power, soul-stirring napalm guitars that laid the groundwork for an entire generation of future punk minimalists. And while their take on the Velvet Underground's *Waiting For The Man* owed at least a little of its arrangement to the version Bowie and Ronson were carrying round the clubs during 1971-72, it was another cover, Kasenatz-Katz's *Quick Joey Small*, which boasted Ronson's liquid lead.

Quick Joey Small became the Slaughter's next single in spring 1978. It was, however, to be this line-up's final offering. Barrett quit in June, around the same time as Decca dropped the group. The group broke up soon after, but by September were back together again, replacing Barrett with ex-Nosebleeds' frontman Ed Banger (a young and unknown Morrissey was also considered for the vacancy.)

Over the next year, Slaughter and the Dogs released three further singles to no more effect than before. Muffet departed, so did Banger. With Rossi taking over vocals, future Cult guitarist Billy Duffy and ex-Eater drummer Phil Rowland stepped into the band, but nothing worked, not even a name change to Slaughter. By mid-1980 they were gone — but not forgotten. Of course their name alone was memorable enough to ensure repeated mentions in sundry Rock and Roll Ripley's Believe It Or Not type features. Less well-recalled, but deserving of more, would be Rossi's own next project, the Duellists, described by Melody Maker as the ultimate "purveyors of passion and personality." "I was sitting at home looking at some old Rolling Stones records one day," Rossi revealed, "and I thought to myself, 'one of us has got to go'."

In later years, Rossi relocated to Los Angeles, moving onto the session scene with startling aplomb. He also convened a mid-1990's Slaughter reunion.

SLAUGHTER AND THE DOGS DISCOGRAPHY
Singles
- *Cranked Up Really High* / *The Bitch* (Rabid TOSH 101, 1977)
- *Where Have All The Boot Boys Gone?* / *You're A Bore* (Decca F13723, 1977)
- *Dame To Blame* / *Johnny T* (Decca F13743, 1977)
- *Quick Joey Small* / *Come On Back* (Decca F13758, 1978)
- *You're Ready Now* / *Runaway* (DJM 10927, 1978)
- BUILD UP NOT DOWN EP: *It's Alright* / *Edgar Allan Poe* / *Twist And Turn* / *UFO* (TJM 3, 1979)
- HALF ALIVE EP: *Twist And Turn* / *Cranked Up Really High* / *Where Have All The Boot Boys Gone?* (Thrush 1, 1983)

Albums
- DO IT DOG-STYLE (Decca SKL 5292, 1978)
- LIVE SLAUGHTER RABID DOGS (Rabid HAT 23, 1978)
- LIVE AT THE FACTORY (Thrush 1, 1978)
- BITE BACK (DJM 20566, 1980)

⋘ **18** ⋙
The Slits

Though the group formed in January 1977 around 14 year old Ari Upp (vocals), Palmolive (drums), ex-Castrators guitarist Kate Korus (rhythm guitar) and Suzi Gutsy (bass), by the time the Slits were ready to reveal themselves, Gutsy had been replaced by another Castrator, Tessa, with Viv Albertine joining from Sid Vicious' rehearsal room-rockers Flowers Of Romance (where she'd played alongside Palmolive) shortly after.

"It wasn't until I saw the Pistols that I realized what I'd been missing," Tessa recalled, "and why I hadn't been to a rock concert for a year. I'd look through the papers and there was nothing I'd want to see. I wanted to buy records but I couldn't find any I wanted to spend money on. And I couldn't understand why. Then when I saw the Pistols, I knew."

Opening their account supporting The Clash at the Harlesden Colosseum in March 1977, the Slits came to national prominence when their presence on The Clash's White Riot tour (alongside The Buzzcocks and Subway Sect) inspired Britain's shock horror gutter press to new heights of verbal dismal — "ALL GIRL PUNK SHOCKERS!" screamed the headlines, and across the country, fathers chained up their daughters and warned then, "Well, you're not joining a band, my girl."

The group's live shows were cacophonous hellfire, the ultimate test of the liberated Rock and Roll critic. When Rolling Stone visited London in August 1977, anxious to get the lowdown on this new punk rock business, a Slits show at the Vortex prompted a dismissive description of a group whose flailings "any current American audience would reward with a shower of bottles," although their inadequacies are excused with a quote from Ari — "Fuckin' shit!' We never said we were musicians.'"

"No, we're not," Viv explained in an interview with UK journalist Caroline Coon. "And that's not cos we can't play brilliantly. It's because if we do [consider ourselves musicians], we know it will be misrepresented. We've heard about musicians! And anyway, is what we play music? Bollocks!"

The Slits remained a musical mess for much of the year — a decade later, Glen Matlock was still grumbling, "They were trying to do the same thing as [the Pistols] but they didn't succeed because they couldn't play." But a Peel session in September 1977 would be repeated five times over the next three months, such was the excitement it generated, a reaction which, in turn, prompted the Slits to spend a little more time refining their live performance.

When the Slits re-emerged early in 1978, even ZigZag's Kris Needs, surely their staunchest journalistic supporter, was moved to write, "Viv's guitar has gained a lot of melody and dynamics, but retains that nerve shredding metallic edge, while Tessa just gets better all the time on bass. She locks in with lethal effect with the powerhouse drumming of Palmolive, who still whacks 'em as hard as anybody, but has stepped up her time-keeping so she now sounds like a cross between Sly and Gary Glitter's two drummers rolled into one."

In fact, Palmolive was not long for the band. Disagreeing with her colleagues' decision to look actively for a major record deal, she quit (for The Raincoats) shortly before the group set out on The Clash's 1978 Sort It Out tour. She was replaced by Big In Japan drummer Budgie. "It was mental," he remembers, "a mental tour. The Clash were filming RUDE BOY, we were staying in small hotels, The Clash were playing the full on rock band, four star hotels, the lot. And I was going 'what is all this?' It was a real eye opening experience."

Through the summer of 1978, there was talk of the group signing with Real Records. In the end it was Island who became the lucky, if somewhat surprising, groom and, early in the new year, work began on the Slits' debut album. By now, their repertoire was vast enough for a double, but while Melody Maker suggested their unique cover of *I Heard It Through The Grapevine* as a single, the band simply noted the songs which, dropped from the set, would not be appearing on the record — *Number One Enemy, Do The Split, Slime, Social Servant, Vaseline, Vindictive,* "they'll obviously come out in the future," Albertine added reassuringly. But not now.

CUT emerged an uncompromising, slavering mass of loose rhythms, lava shrieking and molten riffs, vaguely reggae, pointedly punky and unabashedly unrefined. From the topless mud-wrestlers delight that was the photo session for the album's eventual sleeve, through to the sheer majesty of the sound they conspired to create with producer Dennis Bovell, CUT first shocked, then stunned, then overwhelmed.

Budgie himself later admitted, "I still listen to CUT, and still love it. It was totally crazed, and it worked. The next thing I remember which caught me like that was the first PIL album, where you went 'whoops, what's this sound? What's all this about?'"

Wisely, *Typical Girls* was pulled as the first single, a choice which garnered a lot of airplay and which, even amongst ardent Slits-haters, is the one song which can be played without unpleasantry. The B-side, their so distinctive rendering of *I Heard It Through The Grapevine,* also received a lot of attention (particularly in the US), and was itself to reach an even greater audience when it turned up on a post-punk covers compilation, WE DID 'EM OUR WAY.

CUT breached the UK Top 30, *Typical Girls* the Top 60 and, if either Island or the group had had a mind to it, the Slits might have become the new Blondie, skipping across the TOP OF THE POPS studio, churning out their blistered messages of love and alienation for all eternity.

Instead, they left Island and there was nothing more than a tour which at last found them headlining venues they had previously only come second at, with veteran trumpet player Don Cherry an honorary Slit. And once that was over, it was as if the album . . . the hits . . . the brink of stardom . . . had never happened.

In March, 1980, the Slits resurfaced with a new 45 on Rough Trade. Just six months had elapsed since CUT, but the sound was changing again, the reggae influences so apparent before were now overwhelming, but packaged with a musical stability which countered the band's still eclectic sense of timing with a solid sense of direction.

Only one Slits' track, the self-explanatory *In The Beginning There Was Rhythm*, appeared on the single. The flip, *Where There's A Will, There's A Way* was supplied by labelmates The Pop Group — they would also guest on the group's next release, a cover of reggae great John Holt's masterpiece of conspiratorial paranoia, *Man Next Door*. Hopes for a swift (or even listenable) follow-up to CUT, however, were dismissed when the band instead approved THE OFFICIAL BOOTLEG, a ten track retrospective combining early live and demo work.

Upp later admitted that this period "was survival, really. I never felt with Rough Trade or for Rough Trade. It was the money." Albertine agreed, "it was a matter of handing over something just to get a bit of money back that day. We had nothing." A union with Human Records, for the *Animal Space* single, falls into a similar category. By mid-1981, however, the Slits were back on course. Budgie had quit, to be replaced by Bruce Smith (ex-Pop Group) and, with keyboard player Steve Beresford also on board, the group signed with CBS and commenced work on their second "real" album, RETURN OF THE GIANT SLITS.

Previewed with a single of *Earth Beat* RETURN was launched with the band's insistence that, "we can probably do what we imagine more now" — a terrifying manifesto which swiftly proved to be the case. With the group insisting that both 1978 and 1979 were "just vile memories which aren't even in our heads anymore", the album's reference points were in the same atmospheric free form reggae / funk vein as PIL had most successfully recreated on METAL BOX. But it moved far beyond even those realms, to preface so much of what would become musically current in the late 1980's and early 1990's that it's hard to believe there's a soul in the modern music industry who didn't grow up on the album's turbulent rhythms.

Peter Gabriel, Kate Bush, Bill Laswell, David Byrne, Mr. Sting, all should bow down to the might of the Giant Slits. In fact, few of them have probably even heard them — the album was barely on the streets before the Slits split up. It has never appeared on CD. It's never namedropped in discussions on the most important albums ever made. But it should be, because it was, even if it had left 1977 and punk rock far, far behind it.

Indeed, Upp herself admitted, as RETURN OF THE GIANT SLITS was released, "The Roxy, in the first month, is a good memory, but it's just a dinosaur memory now. [But] we wouldn't hang out with us if we met each other in '77. If these girls five years ago were brought to me now, I reckon I wouldn't be able to communicate. None of us would . . ." They communicated at the time, however, and communicated well. The world would truly have been a poorer place without them.

THE SLITS DISCOGRAPHY

UK Singles

- *Typical Girls / Heard It Through The Grapevine* (Island WIP 6505, 1979)
- *Typical Girls / Heard It Through The Grapevine / Typical Girls* (Brink Style) / *Liebe and Romance* (12") (Island 12WIP 6505, 1979)
- *In The Beginning There Was Rhythm* / Pop Group cut (Rough Trade RT 36, 1980)
- *Man Next Door* / dub version (Y 4, 1980)
- *Animal Space / Animal Spacer* (Human HUM 4, 1980)
- *Earth Beat / Begin Again Rhythm* (CBS A1498, 1981)
- *Earth Beat / Begin Again Rhythm / Earthdub* (12") (CBS A121498, 1981)
- PEEL SESSION EP: *Love & Romance / New Town / Vindictive / Shoplifting* (Strange Fruit SFSP 21, 1987)

US Singles

- *Typical Girls / I Heard It Through The Grapevine* (Antilles, 1979)
- *Man Next Door / In The Beginning / Animal Space* (Human YUS 1, 1980)
- *Earthbeat / Earthdub / Or What Is It?* (Epic 49-02576, 1981)

UK Albums

- CUT (Island ILPS 9573, 1979)
- RETROSPECTIVE — OFFICIAL BOOTLEG (Y 3, 1980)
- RETURN OF THE GIANT SLITS (CBS 85269, 1981)
- THE PEEL SESSIONS (Strange Fruit, 1999)

US Albums

- CUT (Antilles 7072, 1979)
- IN THE BEGINNING (Cleopatra CLP 0065, 1997)

⋘ 19 ⋙
Wire

Manhandled by Menswear, eulogized by Elastica and, for a few months in the mid-1990's, positively everyone's favorite name-dropping drama, Wire sat so uncomfortably in the midst of the punk movement that their very existence, not to mention the hot, harsh nights they put in at the Roxy Club, seemed somehow out of place ... out of time ... out of all logical comprehension. Vocalist Colin Newman once described the group "as a room which people walk in and out of as they see fit. When all of us are in there, then maybe we'll do something." What they did was set a lot of people's teeth on edge ... in the nicest possible way.

Pledging their aural heart to a minimalism that made The Ramones sound like a symphony orchestra, Wire existed around abrupt riffs, staccato vocals, spitting percussion. Onstage, their physical and musical jerking had an intensity which left even the ever present faithful reeling — on vinyl, across their debut album, Wire slammed through 21 songs in less than 40 minutes, but each was so complete that the brevity was barely even noticeable.

Colin Newman (guitar, vocals), Bruce Gilbert (guitar), Graham Lewis (bass, vocals), George Gill (keyboards) and Robert Gotobed (drums) formed Wire in 1976, deliberate amateurs whose reputation for experimentation was, in fact, drawn from their own wish to find out things like, what happens if you put your finger here? They learned quickly, though. A handful of early shows around London caught them opening for The Jam and The Derelicts before Gill departed. In early April 1977, the four piece line-up made their debut (with a brand new set) at the Roxy Punk Festival, a date recorded for the LIVE AT THE ROXY album. Their inexperience didn't show — when the album was released weeks later, they were arguably the most proficient band in sight.

Harvest, the label responsible for the ROXY album, immediately offered Wire a two single contract and, in September, their debut 45, *Mannequin*, proved that the electrifying Roxy noise was not a fluke. Wire really did sing that strangely, perform that jerkily and, as it transpired, play that fast. Although Gotobed later confessed that their most maniacal performance, *12XU*, really was the "the edge of how fast I could play," Wire went into the studio to cut a single and emerged with an entire album, the remarkable PINK FLAG.

The quartet had played no more than six gigs when they went in. They came out and were thrust onto a UK tour with visiting US glam metal wackos the Tubes. They headlined their own outing in the spring, then hit the US that summer. The experience paid off as well — already the group's sound was changing. New material was flooding through, beginning with the minor hits *I Am The Fly* and *Dot Dash*, and culminating in the fall release of their second album, CHAIRS MISSING.

What distinguished Wire more than anything, perhaps, was the fact that their music was so damned catchy. Other bands — The Fall, and the slowly emergent Pop Group and Gang Of Four among them — were also making dense sonic demands upon their listener's attention. But with only a handful of probably accidental exceptions, those demands included a near-complete dismissal of anything that sounded even remotely like a pop tune.

Wire, possibly facetiously, and certainly aggressively, couldn't help but write pop tunes, pop lyrics even. But the execution, the speed, the realization that beneath every sing-along chorus there was a tin full of startled insects buzzing angrily around, all conspired to render Wire a more subversive soul than any of their similarly genre-busting contemporaries.

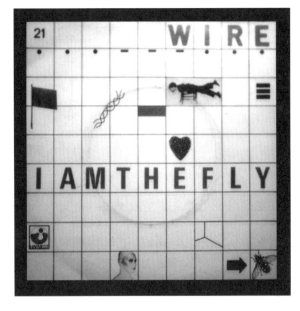

How long could they keep it up for? Not long. Another headline UK tour was followed by a European outing with Roxy Music — one of the few groups from the past with whom Wire could reasonably be compared, but who themselves were already hellbent on pursuing a considerably less fractious course than they had. The tour was miserable, Wire were losing faith.

154, Wire's third album, in September 1979, would be their last — it was followed, within months, by the band's weary admission that they had finally exhausted the pool of ideas which once sustained them. A string of solo activities awaited, spread across the next six years and, while Wire would reformed in 1986, again it was for just three albums in a totally different direction to before. Drummer Gotobed quit, leaving his bandmates to continue briefly as Wir. By 1991, that, too, had fizzled out, and it would be close to a decade later before the classic Wire reunited, for UK and US tours during the spring of 2000.

WIRE DISCOGRAPHY
UK Singles
- *Mannequin / Feeling Called Love / 12Xu* (Harvest HAR 5144, 1977)
- *I Am the Fly / Ex-Lion Tamer* (Harvest HAR 5151, 1978)
- *Dot Dash / Options* (Harvest HAR 5161, 1978)
- *Outdoor Miner / Practice Makes Perfect* (Harvest HAR 5172, 1979)
- *A Question Of Degree / Former Airline* (Harvest HAR 5187, 1979)
- *Map Ref 41N 93W / Go Ahead* (Harvest HAR 5192, 1979)

○ *The Peel Sessions (1191978)* (Strange Fruit 041, 1987)

UK Albums
  ○ PINK FLAG (Harvest SHSP 4076, 1977)
  ○ CHAIRS MISSING (Harvest SHSP 4093, 1979)
  ○ 154 (Harvest SHSP 4105, 1979)
  ○ DOCUMENT & EYEWITNESS (live 1979) (Rough Trade ROUGH 29, 1981)
  ○ THE PEEL SESSIONS (Strange Fruit SFRCD 108, 1989)
  ○ ON RETURNING 1977-79 (Restless 72358, 1989)

◄ **20** ►
X-Ray Spex

Marion Elliot had already released one single, *Silly Billy*, as a schoolgirl solo singer by the time she formed X-Ray Spex. Now working on the candy counter at a branch of Woolworths, she placed a musicians wanted ad in Melody Maker in the summer of 1976 after seeing The Sex Pistols show at Hastings Pavilion. It paid immediate dividends in the form of Jak "Airport" Stafford, bassist Paul Dean, drummer Chris Chrysler and 15 year old Susan Whitby (sax.) In keeping with the times, the women, at least, adopted new names — Poly Styrene (Elliot), Laura Logic (Whitby) — before launching themselves onto the London club scene early in the new year.

Fortunate to land a near-residency at the Man In The Moon pub in Chelsea, X-Ray Spex had played exactly one show before appearing at the Roxy. There, the highlight of their short set, Styrene's *Oh Bondage! Up Yours*, was recorded for the LIVE AT THE ROXY album, a discordant duet for shriek and saxophone, while the group buzzed busily in the background.

Both EMI and Virgin were keen to sign the band — Virgin won out with an offer for a one-off single, again of *Oh Bondage*. It was a tremendous record, flying in the face of all conventional musical wisdom . . . style . . . form . . . tunefulness, but managing to hold all four together even as Styrene warbled, Logic blasted and the group went into gratuitous meltdown. Whatever else X-Ray Spex might achieve, *Oh Bondage* had already done more than most groups manage in an entire career.

But X-Ray Spex were more, far more, than a simple one song pony. Drawn from the band's demos, a nine track bootleg, containing studio versions of the essential elements of the combo's live set, did the rounds to ever growing support and, with Poly's own persona proving ever more fascinating to the media, X-Ray Spex became one of the star attractions of the Hope & Anchor's Front Row Festival.

The group departed Virgin at year's end and moved across to EMI. The simultaneous departure of Logic (for her own cacophony, Essential Logic) would, with hindsight, strip some of the visceral immediacy from the band's sound, but still their new suitors could only marvel at what they'd gotten their hands on. Espousing a philosophy half condemning, half admiring modern trash culture, Styrene was developing into an admirable eccentric. Her songs obsessed on personal hygiene and the lore of litter; she in turn littered her lyrics with references to consumerism's crassest triumphs — irresistible fodder for the marketing department. Spex's first EMI single, March, 1978's *The World Turned Day-Glo*, was released in near day-glo orange vinyl. What else?

It became an immediate Top 30 single, even as X-Ray Spex crossed the ocean for a sold out six nights at CBGBs. They returned home for the Rock Against Racism gig at Victoria Park, Hackney, then slammed out their next 45, the visceral screech of *Identity*.

Styrene, meanwhile, continued to intrigue the media and, as it transpired, baffle her fans and fellows. She spoke enthusiastically of the need for "natural" living, which was fair enough. But then she started talking (in an interview with the tabloid Daily Mirror) of the pink flying saucer whose crew instructed her to warn the world of the dangers of "the synthetic life," shortly before holing up at manager Falcon Stuart's house and refusing to venture outside.

Working around Styrene's oddity, X-Ray Spex completed their debut album for a November 1978 release. It was previewed by a single of the title track, *Germ Free Adolescents*, a winsome collision between the Who's *Baba O'Reilly* and a deodorant commercial, and accompanied, at last, by X-Ray Spex's first full UK tour. At last . . . and alas. The album was a disappointment, pointedly over-produced and bereft of both the mad spontaneity of the group's best singles and the spont-

X-Ray Spex

aneous madness which had marked them out as special a mere year or so ago. Indeed, even the group's staunchest supporters were disappointed, yearning instead for vinyl which recaptured the true joy of Spex ... the live *Let's Submerge* ... the four track John Peel session aired earlier in the year ... the concert footage which TV's OMNIBUS procured from a Liverpool gig for use in the documentary WHO IS POLY STYRENE? They never got it and never would. Barely was the tour complete than rumors of an X-Ray split began flying.

The end finally came in Paris that May, when Styrene announced that she wanted the band to play slower, gentler music. Her bandmates disagreed and that was it. Styrene ventured into a fitful solo career, but preferred to remain out of sight for much of the next two years. The rest of Spex tried to carry on without her, but a series of auditions turned up no suitable replacements, and they finally broke up in August.

Neither did a Spex reunion in 1995 deliver anywhere near the promise it initially held — Styrene, Dean and Logic were all on board for the CONSCIOUS CONSUMER album, but sales were poor and, when a planned appearance at the 1996 Holidays In The Sun punk festival passed off without Styrene's attendance, it was clear that again, the project had run its course.

X-RAY SPEX DISCOGRAPHY
UK Singles
- *Oh Bondage! Up Yours! / I Am A Cliche* (Virgin VS 189, 1977)
- *World Turned Day-glo / IAMA Poseur* (EMI INT 553, 1978)
- *Identity / Let's Submerge* (EMI INT 563, 1978)
- *Germ Free Adolescents / Age* (EMI INT 573, 1978)
- *Highly Inflammable / Warrior In Woolworths* (EMI INT 583, 1979)

UK Albums
- GERM FREE ADOLESCENTS (EMI Int 3023, 1978)
- LIVE AT THE ROXY (different, full show) (Receiver RRCD 140, 1991)
- OBSESSED WITH YOU (Receiver RRCD 145, 1991)
- GERM FREE ADOLESCENTS (Virgin CDVM 9001, 1992)

≪ Part Three ≫
— Old Enough To Know Better —

≪ 21 ≫
Elvis Costello And The Attractions

The son of jazz bandleader Ross McManus, Declan "Elvis Costello" McManus shoved himself onto the scene at a time when even punk's fieriest acolytes were seeking that most elusive of musical properties — the next Bob Dylan. The Pistols, The Damned and most especially The Clash had, after all, already sewn up most of the new era's other iconographical vacancies, but a distinctly unwilling Graham Parker notwithstanding, the role of Bitter Laureate remained unclaimed. Then Stiff Records unearthed the highly literate, astonishingly lyrical and utterly curmudgeonly Costello, and all was right with the world.

Having come to the label's attention after submitting demos of his last group, Flip City, Costello recorded his debut album in 24 hours in early 1977, with backing from visiting American country rockers Clover (featuring Huey Lewis) and production from Nick Lowe, Stiff house producer and a graduate from another of the pub rock underground's most venerable titans, Brinsley Schwarz. Together, the team concocted MY AIM IS TRUE, one of the angriest, yet understated, albums of the year, a set which did indeed live up to the Dylan tag, but only in terms of its bile. Musically, lyrically and creatively, it was its own beast entirely.

The press went nuts for Costello from the start. The public was a little slower. Three early singles did nothing, but with the semi-anthemic *(The Angels Wanna Wear My) Red Shoes* coming close, by the time MY AIM IS TRUE was released that July, a Top 20 berth awaited. *Watching The Detectives,*

Elvis Costello And The Attractions

CAMBRIDGE CORN EXCHANGE
Friday 31st MARCH

elvis costello
and the attractions
Plus Guests

Advance ticket £2.00
Doors open 8.00 pm

Nº 000543

Costello's first release with his now-regular backing group, the Attractions, was the breakthrough.

With Steve Nieve's keyboard now the dominant musical feature, Costello traded the wiry nervousness of his early sound for a dark, often malevolent punch — *Detectives*, laced around a sub dub bass riff, an earthy post Doors muddiness and superbly cinematic lyrics, made No. 20 in October, even as the unit took their show on the road as part of the much (and deservedly) hyped Live Stiffs tour. Alongside Ian Dury, Nick Lowe, Wreckless Eric and Larry Wallis, this return to the decade of old days of package tours would make stars of all three headliners, and cults of both Eric and Wallis, with the most enduring memory of Costello's show being, again, the sheer impact of the Attractions' sound.

November saw MY AIM IS TRUE make it out in the US in a markedly different version to the UK release, but it immediately became apparent that Costello's early American career was never going to move as straightforwardly as its UK counterpart. His first Stateside release, the caustic *Alison*, was irrevocably sweetened first by Columbia's decision to add strings to the brew, then when Linda Ronstadt picked it up for a cover — Costello was apparently furious about both, and vented at least some of his spleen when he appeared on SATURDAY NIGHT LIVE at the end of the year, replacing the visa-ensnared Sex Pistols.

The ensuing publicity, coupled with Costello's willingness to tour until his legs fell off, paid off. THIS YEAR'S MODEL, Costello and the Attractions' first album together, breached the American Top 30, while a triptych of thunderously apocalyptic singles, *(I Don't Want To Go To) Chelsea*, *Pump It Up* and *Radio Radio*, all hit the British Top 30.

Although Costello and the Attractions have continued working together, at least sporadically, ever since, there is no denying that this initial burst of activity remains their finest hour, a point proven first by the continued run of singly excellent singles they were unleashing; secondly, by their live shows (we all know bootlegs are naughty, but everyone needs a '78-era Elvis one); and finally, by the unadulterated majesty of their next album, ARMED FORCES.

Released in January 1979, ARMED FORCES presented an airier vista than its predecessor, at least in sonic terms. Lyrically, however, Costello remained as snipingly potent as ever, as his original title for the record, EMOTIONAL FASCISM, suggested. Yet there was a lightening of the fury in the wind and, as the 1970's gave way to a new decade, so the Attractions fell by the wayside briefly, allowing Costello the luxury of a "solo" album, 1980's GET HAPPY. And get happy (-er), of course, was pretty much what he did, spreading his musical wings to embrace both personal and musical emotions which had only been flashed upon in the past.

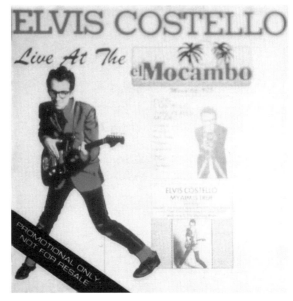

Costello moved away from his punk / new wave roots at the speed of light. Moved away, too, from the last vestiges of the Dylan hangover, towards a position more fondly associated with Van Morrison. Of course it was a smart move — it's his refusal to either stand still, or compromise while he is on the run, which has ensured Costello's longevity; and his ability to continually surprise listeners (and possibly, himself) which means he remains worth listening to.

ELVIS COSTELLO AND THE ATTRACTIONS DISCOGRAPHY (1977-79)
UK Singles
- *Less Than Zero / Radio Sweetheart* (Stiff BUY 11, 1977)
- *Alison / Welcome To The Working Week* (Stiff BUY 14, 1977)
- *Red Shoes / Mystery Dance* (Stiff BUY 15, 1977)
- *Watching The Detectives / Blame It On Cain / Mystery Dance* (Stiff BUY 20, 1977)
- *Chelsea / You Belong To Me* (Radar ADA 3, 1978)
- *Stranger In The House / Neat Neat Neat* (Radar SAM 83, 1978)
- *Pump It Up / Big Tears* (Radar ADA 10, 1978)
- *Radio Radio / Tiny Steps* (Radar ADA 24, 1978)
- *Peace, Love & Understanding /* Nick Lowe cut (Radar ADA 26, 1978)
- *Talking In The Dark / Wednesday Week* (Radar RG 1, 1978)
- *Oliver's Army / My Funny Valentine* (Radar ADA 31, 1979)
- LIVE AT HOLLYWOOD HIGH EP: *Accidents Will Happen / Watching The Detectives / Alison* (Radar SAM 90, 1979)
- *Accidents Will Happen / Talking In The Dark / Wednesday Week* (Radar ADA 35, 1979)

US Singles
- *Alison / Miracle Man* (Columbia 10641, 1988)
- *Watching The Detectives / Alison* (Columbia 10705, 1977)
- *This Year's Girl / Big Tears* (Columbia 10762, 1978)

UK Albums
- MY AIM IS TRUE (Stiff SEEZ 3, 1977)
- THIS YEAR'S MODEL (Radar RAD 3, 1978)

∘ ARMED FORCES (Radar RAD 15, 1979)
∘ TEN BLOODY MARYS & TEN HOWS YOUR FATHERS (compilation)
  (F Beat XXC 6, 1980)
∘ TWO AND A HALF YEARS (boxed-set) (Demon DPAM BOX 1, 1993)

US Albums
∘ MY AIM IS TRUE (Columbia 35037, 1977)
∘ THIS YEAR'S MODEL (Columbia 35331, 1978)
∘ ARMED FORCES (Columbia 35709, 1979)
∘ TAKING LIBERTIES (compilation) (Columbia 36839, 1980)
∘ TWO AND A HALF YEARS (boxed-set) (Rykodisc 20271-4, 1993)

⪪ 22 ⪫
Ian Dury

He died, said his family, as he lived — with a smile on his face, from an illness which he'd known for two years would eventually get the better of him. But still the passing of Ian Dury, from inoperable liver cancer on March 27, 2000, was shocking enough that, even without a hit in 20 years, it made the front page of Britain's traditionally staid Daily Telegraph and Independent newspapers, while almost every commentator titled his coverage after one of Dury's greatest hits, *What A Waste*. And they were right.

A Rock and Roll superstar who doubled as the last of Britain's great vaudeville entertainers, Dury was born in Upminster, London, on May 12, 1942 — "conceived at the back of the Ritz," he later remarked, "and born at the height of the Blitz." He was seven when he contracted polio at an open air swimming pool at the seaside resort of Southend. His was one of nine cases reported and, initially, he was not expected to survive more than six months — with uncanny symmetry, Dury's doctor gave him precisely the same grim forecast back in January, 1998, when cancer was first detected in his liver. By then, however, Dury had turned beating the odds into an artform.

Polio rendered Dury temporarily paralyzed and left him with a lifelong limp. He was a gifted artist, however, and by 1960 was studying under Peter Blake at Walthamstow School of Art. He did some magazine illustrations and, within a decade, he was lecturing at Canterbury College of Art.

It was there that he met the musicians who would join him in his first group, Kilburn And The High Roads, in 1970. An artful blend of American funk and English music hall, with Dury a misfit who apparently revelled in his disability, the Kilburns lasted six years and two albums — one, in 1974, shelved when their label (Warners subsidiary Raft) went under; the second, HANDSOME, released the following year to great reviews but poor sales. The Kilburns finally broke up in summer, 1976 — the opening act at their farewell show was The Sex Pistols.

Dury resurfaced the following year, signed now to ex-Kilburns' manager Dave Robinson's Stiff label. But in an age dominated by punk, few observers gave a 35 year old crippled ex-schoolteacher a hope in hell. Which was precisely the kind of challenge Dury relished. Scrapping a high sheen dance set which was intended as his Stiff debut album, Dury and writing partner Chaz Jankel instead went back to basics, adopting a loose, un-produced and raw-nerved shuffle, then slammed it out as Dury's debut single, the immortal mantra of SEX AND DRUGS AND ROCK AND ROLL.

Released in August 1977, SEX AND DRUGS was wholeheartedly embraced by the new punk community and the reasons were not hard to discern. In a musical form which prided itself on its Englishness (as opposed to the Americanisms, or even Trans-Atlanticisms of most other existing styles), Dury was unquestionably homegrown, spitting colloquialisms like machine gun fire, honoring forgotten music hall heroes in speech and in song, wearing his eccentricities like a badge.

Certainly they were spattered throughout NEW BOOTS AND PANTIES!!, the debut album by Dury and his newly formed Blockheads. Songs like *Billericay Dickie*, *Clever Trevor*, *Plaistow Patricia* and *Blockheads* itself may have had little in common with the adrenalin rush of "pure" punk, but they lurched with a dyspeptic defiance which left younger acts trailing helplessly in Dury's wake — as the Blockheads proved with a co-headlining spot on the fall 1977 Live Stiffs tour.

NEW BOOTS AND PANTIES!! would remain on the UK charts for nearly two years, eventually

Ian Dury

selling over a million copies worldwide. A new single, *What A Waste*, made the Top 10 in early 1978. But the Blockheads had barely begun their rise. By the end of the year the riotously pun-packed *Hit Me With Your Rhythm Stick* had climbed to No. 1 and, while attempts to launch Dury in the US proved less than even marginally successful, in Europe, he could do no wrong.

Or could he? DO IT YOURSELF, Dury's second album, was an immediate hit, but a critical turkey, as the increasingly ambitious Blockheads attempted to add disco funk to their musical stew and smooth out some of the rough edges which had made PANTIES!! so remarkable. A Top 3 single, *Reasons to Be Cheerful (Part 3)*, went some way towards disguising the rot, but when the DIY tour wrapped up, so did Dury's relationship with Jankel. The latter quit, to be replaced by former Dr. Feelgood hero Wilko Johnson, and 1980 brought the final Blockheads' album, the less-than-superlative LAUGHTER.

Dury launched a solo career — which itself would only lurch sporadically through the 1980's, while the singer occupied himself with a new career in cinema, theater and television voice-overs. He appeared in Polanski's THE PIRATES, Dylan's HEARTS OF FIRE and Bob Hoskyns' THE RAGGEDY RAWNEY, among others. The death (also from cancer) of Blockheads' drummer Charley Charles, in September 1990, drew Dury back to regular performance as the surviving Blockheads reconvened to play a benefit for Charles' family, captured on 1991's WARTS AND AUDIENCE live album. Further concerts followed, together with Dury's own BUS DRIVER'S HOLIDAY album (1992.)

Dury was diagnosed with colon cancer in 1995, little more than a year after the death, again from cancer, of his first wife, Betty (the pair separated in 1985.) The news didn't slow him down. Though it would be 1998 before his next album, the reconvened Blockheads' drolly titled MR LOVE PANTS, Dury was now gigging regularly — remarkably, he played his final show just two weeks before his death.

He was visibly weakening, however. Several dates on a 1999 festival tour with fellow Stiff Records alumnus (Wreckless) Eric Goulden, were cancelled, while it was touch and go whether he would even be able to attend the Q magazine awards, shortly before Christmas 1999, where he was to be presented with the Classic Songwriter award. He did get there in the end, to be feted by an entire generation of English musicians whose own work was unquestionably informed by Dury's work.

Madness, Blur and Carter USM are just three of the chart-toppers whose musical (and, especially, lyrical) roots can be traced back to NEW BOOTS AND PANTIES, *Rhythm Stick* and the Kilburns, just as Dury's can be traced back to an even earlier, but equally unique age, the days of the Max's Wall and Miller, Alma Cogan, Flanders and Swann and, of course, "Sweet" Gene Vincent, the 50's Rock and Roller whose own life and legend was the subject of a Dury song as touching as any he ever wrote — and would stand as poignantly appropriate to his own memory today as it was to Vincent's back then.

IAN DURY AND THE BLOCKHEADS DISCOGRAPHY
UK Singles
- *Sex And Drugs And Rock And Roll / Razzle In My Pocket* (Stiff BUY 17, 1977)
- *Sex & Drugs / Two Steep Hills / England's Glory* (Stiff FREEB 3, 1977)
- *Sweet Gene Vincent / You're More Than Fair* (Stiff BUY 23, 1977)
- *What A Waste / Wake Up!* (Stiff BUY 27, 1978)
- *Hit Me With Your Rhythm Stick / Clever Bastards* (Stiff BUY 38, 1978)
- *Reasons To Be Cheerful Pt 3 / Common As Muck* (Stiff BUY 50, 1979)
- *I Want To Be Straight / That's Not All* (Stiff BUY 90, 1980)
- *Sueperman's Big Sister / You'll See Glimpses* (Stiff BUY 100, 1980)
- *Sueperman's Big Sister / Fuckin' Ada* (Stiff BUYIT 100, 1981)

UK Albums
- NEW BOOTS & PANTIES!! (Stiff SEEZ 4, 1977)
- DO IT YOURSELF (Stiff SEEZ 14, 1979)
- LAUGHTER (Stiff SEEZ 30, 1981)
- JUKE BOX DURY (Stiff SEEZ 41, 1981)
- SEX AND DRUGS AND ROCK AND ROLL (Demon FIEND 69, 1987)
- IAN DURY AND THE BLOCKHEADS (boxed-set) (Demon IAN 1, 1991)

US Albums
- NEW BOOTS & PANTIES (Stiff 002, 1978)
- DO IT YOURSELF (Stiff 36104, 1979)
- LAUGHTER (Stiff 36998, 1981)

⇇ 23 ⇉
The Maniacs

Of all the groups that emerged during the hectic summer of 1976, few were quite so — eccentric? Peculiar? Deliberately weird? as the Maniacs. A duo comprising guitarist Alan Lee Shaw and drummer Rod Latter, ten years earlier they could have given Marc Bolan's Tyrannosaurus Rex a run for their sugar lumps. In the days of punk, however, they were unique and, when ex-Pink Fairy Twink decided to dip his toes into the scene, it was the Maniacs to whom he turned, changing their name to the Rings and taking them to the 1977 Mont de Marsen punk festival.

Shaw and Latter had been together since 1970, meeting in Germany where their servicemen fathers were stationed. Returning to the UK, their first group, Guts, was succeeded by ZZZ, the space rock freak show that first linked them with Twink — he took the lead vocals spot and led the band onto the prog circuit, supporting the likes of Hawkwind, the Fairies and Edgar Broughton, before quitting on the eve of signing a record contract.

Under Shaw's own name, the surviving duo released a single, *She Moans*, in 1974 — with wholly accidental prescience, the NME review of the record appeared beneath the headline "Punk Rock" and didn't actually mention the song once. It was more concerned with the sexual connotations of the title ("She moans? I bet she does".)

Shaw and Latter became the Maniacs soon after, changing their name in deference to their audience's perceptions of their live show. They also moved to London from their earlier base in Cambridge and worked solidly for the next two years. Twink reappeared in late 1976 and, as the Rings, an impetuously primitive single, *I Wanna Be Free*, was released by Chiswick. It was an uneasy union, however, with Shaw and Latter agitating for more control and Twink demanding total obedience. Finally the singer quit again, this time on the eve of the Mont de Marsen show. Shaw, Latter and bassist Dennis Stowe agreed to play the show alone — only for Twink to turn up with his own, newly convened version of the Rings and play a set as well. The two groups spent the rest of the festival arguing.

Returning home and replacing Stowe with Robert Crash, the group reverted to their earlier name and signed to UA, releasing one single (*Chelsea 77*), but recording close to an album's worth of additional material — the source of the sundry Maniacs collections to have been released in recent years (an LP on Released Emotions in 1990, and a massive CD upgrade eight years later.)

The Maniacs also became a regular sight at the Vortex and a live compilation recorded there in fall 1977 preserves at least a snatch of the group in full demonic flight. By the time the record hit the stores, however, the Maniacs had split, saying goodbye in January 1978.

Crash formed the Psychotic Tanks, whose sole single (produced by Shaw) comes over like a fabulous collision between

Elvis Presley and a bottle of downers. Latter joined the Monotones, before replacing temporary drummer John Towe in The Adverts in the spring of 1978. Shaw formed the Physicals and released the semi-infamous ALL SEXED UP EP.

Other sessions and live recordings followed, eventually captured on the Physicals' SKULDUGGERY compilation. A second single produced by Sex Pistol Paul Cook followed during 1980. *Pain In Love*, however, marked the end of the Physicals, and Shaw linked instead with ex-Damned guitarist Brian James in The All-Stars, an ad hoc act that eventually metamorphosed into Brian James' Brains and later, the Hellions.

The Maniacs reformed for a single show in May 1990, opening for The Lurkers at the London Powerhouse, to coincide with the release of the AIN'T NO LEGEND album. Talk of a tour proved premature, but Shaw remained active, joining first with Brian James for his solo debut album, then enlisting with The Damned for their NOT OF THIS EARTH renaissance. At decade's end, he and another Damned alumni, Paul Gray, were working together as Mischief.

THE MANIACS DISCOGRAPHY
Singles
ALAN LEE SHAW
 ○ *She Moans / Bolweevil* (Alaska 123, 1974)
RINGS
 ○ *I Wanna Be Free / Automobile* (Chiswick NS 14, 1977)
MANIACS
 ○ *Chelsea 77 / Ain't No Legend* (UA UP 36327, 1977)
PHYSICALS
 ○ ALL SEXED UP EP (Physical PR 001, 1978)
 ○ *Pain In Love / Be Like Me* (Big Beat NS 58, 1980)

Albums
MANIACS
  ○ SO FAR SO LOUD (Overground 77, 1998)
PHYSICALS
  ○ SKULDUGGERY (Overground 80, 1999)

≪ **24** ≫
John Otway And Wild Willy Barrett

Frenzied folk punk duo Otway-Barrett had been haunting the nightmare-ridden extremes of the music industry since 1971, a self-confessed madman whose vocal range was placed somewhere between a squeaking bedframe and an enraged elk (Otway) and an unabashed musical genius with an insatiable desire to make his guitar suffer (Barrett.)

Lurching, sometimes literally, out of their Aylesbury home town, Otway, at least, was convinced he was destined to become a superstar. His songwriting (which genuinely was of stellar quality) was single-mindedly self-mythologizing, whether he was projecting the extent of his own future fame (*Geneve*), or contextualizing his own friends and family (*Louisa On A Horse*, *Jet Spotter Of The Track*.) Barrett, on the other hand, claimed he only stayed with Otway because it annoyed the musical snobs who would come to marvel at his technique and ability, then ask why he hung around with the loony.

In 1973, Pete Townshend was sufficiently impressed to sign the duo to Track Records and produce a single with them. On other occasions, the pair released their own 45's, the gentle *Gypsy* in 1972 and the fiendishly manic *Beware Of The Flowers (Cos I'm Sure They're Gonna Get You, Yeah)* in 1975. All un-amped guitar, sibilant hissing, cracking high notes and scorching bongoes, *Flowers* appeared as a limited edition of 500 and was already long sold out by the time Sounds made it their single of the week in June.

Track Records immediately resurfaced, releasing a second single from the Townshend sessions and suggesting the duo cut an entire album, which they would certainly be very interested in hearing. Otway-Barrett leaped to their bidding, combining selected earlier recordings (the Townshend material again included) with more recent studio fare and, in March 1977, delivered the fruits of their labors. Track took one listen, then rejected it. Otway-Barrett responded by releasing OTWAY-BARRETT themselves, on the wryly named Ex-Tracked label.

Immediately, things started moving. The duo shifted 1,000 copies of the album in the first week, selling it at gigs and by mail order. John Peel procured a copy and played four tracks on his show. By July 1977, Track's own distributors, Polydor, were hotly pursuing Otway-Barrett's signature and preparing to reissue the album themselves.

The attention arrived at precisely the right time. Refining a live show which was already the subject of much whispered awe, Otway-Barrett launched now into the development of new heights of onstage abuse. Barrett loved to see Otway hurt himself, Otway apparently loved to get hurt and, with the duo having first drawn a fine line between slapstick humor and gratuitous violence, they then drove a steamroller right across it.

Never one of nature's more finely co-ordinated specimens, Otway threw himself at the live performance in much the same way as a gymnast approaches the climax of an Olympic routine — literally. He would leap from speakers, as though straining for some imaginary bar high above the stage, then plummet earthwards without a care. Man and microphone would investigate one another's most intimate regions — during the showstopping *Down The Road*, it was not at all unusual to find Otway with the mike halfway down his throat, imitating the sounds of young lovers in the throes of vulgar passion. Later, he and Barrett developed a song called *Headbutts*, the point of which was for Barrett to crack his partner on the skull every time the song's title came around. Which was a lot. Even after the high art of punk immolation hit the tabloid headlines, still Otway-Barrett's anarchic brand of nihilistic self-annihilation was in a field of its own — as the world was about to find out.

Their first Polydor single, *Racing Cars* (featuring one of Barrett's finest inventions, a rewired pedal steel guitar which truly did sound like a demolition derby), scored great reviews but sold poorly. Now a new single, the molten fudge fuzzed guitar led *(Cor Baby That's) Really Free* was imminent and with it, a clutch of high profile concerts and TV shows.

A gig at the London Roundhouse, sold out weeks in advance, was recorded for a possible live album (it was eventually released to the fan club only.) Next came slots on TV's SO IT GOES and OLD GREY WHISTLE TEST. *Really Free* was to be the highlight of both, but it was Otway who made the headlines, a gangling freak ricochetting around the stage, contorting face and body into ever more inhuman shapes, while that voice ... that voice ... By late September, *Really Free* was Top 30 bound, with sales of 150,000+.

Otway alone gigged through the end of the year. Barrett was in the studio, reveling in the luxury of having a proper recording budget for the first time in his career, completing the duo's second album. The severance did little to alter Otway's demeanor; even with a backing band of staid session men, he remained a lunatic — as he proved when he chose to follow up the hit with a solo single, a version of the album's *Geneve*, cut with a full orchestra.

It should have been enormous, and most people thought it would be. But Polydor had lost interest already. Neither *Geneve* nor, weeks later, the DEEP AND MEANINGLESS album received any promotion — the label didn't even bother plucking a single from the album, and that despite a good half of the record screaming out for the honor. Matters worsened when Barrett walked out on the duo's next tour, pleading sickness and an uncontrollable urge to watch the soccer World Cup on TV.

Otway promptly convened a new group, slicker than it possibly could have been, but still a vibrant vehicle for the insanity. A new single, *Baby's In The Club*, bombed out, however, and a full solo album, WHERE DID I GO RIGHT?, wound up both impossibly over-produced and dramatically underachieving — the best tracks were ones Otway had been performing for years (most notably a fiery epic recounting of the Alfred, Lord Noyes' classic poem, *The Highwayman*.) The remainder was increasingly wackiness-by-the-numbers. A 1980 reunion with Barrett fared little better and, by the end of the year, Polydor and the madcap duo had finally parted company.

Both parties, however, had got what they wanted — for Otway, a taste of the fame which even his best friends were adamant he would never, ever achieve — twenty years on, he remains an active cult force, regularly recording and gigging while branching out into acting and theater as well. And for Polydor, an utterly memorable, utterly distinctive hit single which could then be stuck onto every punk / new wave themed compilation the label could ever want to produce. Indeed, in the months before The Jam and Sham 69 began delivering, it was the only one they had.

Folkies Otway-Barrett may well have been, but with savage distortion and that maniac of a voice, the pair meshed perfectly with the climate of the time. Up there alongside Gabba Gabba Hey, Bored Teenagers and We're So Pretty ... Really Free, the song and the statement, became one of THE chants of the year, before chants lost their charm, punk lost its teeth and Otway, of course, lost his Willy. And while it can be argued, quite convincingly, that Otway-Barrett themselves fell far beyond even the most generous remit of punk and its possibilities, it is that very isolation that cements their right to be included within it.

OTWAY-BARRETT PUNK YEARS (AND THEREABOUTS) DISCOGRAPHY

Singles
- *Murder Man / If I Did* (Track 2094 111, 1973)
- *Beware Of The Flowers / Louisa On A Horse* (Viking [no catalog No.], 1975)
- *Louisa On A Horse / Misty Mountain* (Track 2094 133, 1976)
- *Racing Cars / Running From The Law* (Polydor 2058 916, 1977)
- *Really Free / Beware Of The Flowers* (Polydor 2058 951, 1977)
- *Racing Cars* (live) / *Down The Road* (live) (free with early pressings of DEEP AND MEANINGLESS LP) (Polydor OT 1, 1978)

Albums
- OTWAY-BARRETT (Extracked EXLP 1, 1977)
- LIVE AT THE ROUNDHOUSE ([white label], 1977)
- OTWAY-BARRETT (Polydor 2383 453, 1977)
- DEEP AND MEANINGLESS (Polydor 2383 501, 1978)

⋖ 25 ⋗
Radio Stars

Jet, the splintered relics of a glam rock past, were no more. Bassist Martin Gordon, who once powered Sparks to the heights of British breakthrough success, was off working with New Yorker Ian North in a new group called Ian's Radio. Guitarist Ian McLeod, who replaced 60's guitar legend Davy O'List in time for Jet's unreleased second album, was a milkman. Drummer Chris Townson, once of 60's psychedelic cult heroes John's Children and 70's skinhead failures Jook, was swearing he would never play in another band again. And vocalist Andy Ellison, also of John's Children, was walking through Camden Town, north London.

"I stopped to look in the Rock On! record shop. It was a total chance thing, but while I was there I remembered hearing there was a small record label upstairs from the shop. I didn't know anything more about it than that, but I decided to go up there anyway."

In his bag, for no apparent reason, he carried a tape, the last will and testament of Jet. It comprised four songs, *Antlers* (about suitcases), *Sail Away* (about escaping), *Don't Cry Joe* (about actress Charlotte Rampling) and *Dirty Pictures* (about dirty pictures.) He handed a copy to the man in the label office, Ted Carroll, head of Chiswick Records, and admits he was surprised by what happened next.

"Ted was really knocked out by *Dirty Pictures*. He wanted to release it right away, but naturally he assumed Martin and I would be wanting to do everything on a big level, which Chiswick could never afford. I finally managed to persuade him that all we wanted was someone who would put a record out for us, and Ted was the first person I'd met who considered anything on the tape to be commercially viable. The money side of things didn't matter to us — we were broke already and we'd carry on being broke, but at least we'd have a record out."

Rather than re-record the songs, thus using up what little budget they did have, Ellison and Gordon opted simply to coax McLeod away from his milk bottles to overdub some new, edgier guitar parts. They remixed *Dirty Pictures* and *Sail Away*, then turned to more pressing problems like — what were they going to call the band? "We had drawn up a shortlist of five possibilities," says Gordon, "and left it with Ted. One day the Melody Maker called him, they'd heard Andy and I had signed to Chiswick, and they wanted to know what the band was called. Ted looked at the list and said 'oh, Radio Stars.' The first we knew about it was when it appeared in the paper."

Dirty Pictures was released on April 8, 1977, an immediate cult classic which, somehow slipping past the BBC censors, found its way onto the JOHN PEEL show and ended up selling enough copies to make the independent / punk charts.

On April 30, 1977, the new group made its live debut (opening for UFO in front of 6,500 rabid German headbangers) with drummer Gary Thompson replacing the still retiring Townson. Eight days later, returning home in triumph, they played their first UK show at a girls' school in Mill Hill, before Thompson departed to form a new group, power pop heroes Tonight. He was replaced by one Paul Simon, a non-small, non-Jewish, non-Homeward Bound gentleman then working with Ian North's latest effort, Neo. Simon would divide his time between the two groups until a major dilemma dawned and he had to choose between touring Japan with Radio Stars and playing the Marquee with Neo. Naturally he chose to play the Marquee.

The Japanese tour was cancelled, but with drummer Jim Toomey standing in, a UK outing with Eddie And The Hot Rods was slipped in as compensation, together with a new single, the immortal STOP IT EP — opening with *No Russians In Russia*, a tribute to US President Ford's insistence that the Eastern Bloc was not controlled by Communists. That fall, Radio Stars made their TV debut on MARC, a weekly TV show hosted by another former John's Children member, Marc Bolan.

Toomey quit to join Annie Lennox and Dave Stewart's pre-Eurythmics outfit, the Tourists. He was replaced by Steve Parry and Radio Stars cut their debut album, provisionally titled BOWELS STUFFED WITH SPLEEN (from a line in the song *Macaroni And Mice*.) Squeamishly, Chiswick pleaded for something a little less unappetizing — the group replaced it with SONGS FOR SWINGING LOVERS, but otherwise their monumental and, admittedly, tongue-in-cheek lack of taste was given full reign, via an ode to a recent serial rapist, *The Beast Of Barnsley*, a tribute to the just-deceased Elvis Presley, *Arthur is Dead Boring (Let's Rot)* and *Nervous Wreck*, positively the finest pop song ever to feature a girlie chorus trilling "electro-encephalograph." That would become Radio Stars' next single and first hit, a Top 30 smash early in the new year.

A second, utterly spectacular tour with Eddie And The Hot Rods took the band through spring 1978, but the inexplicable failure of their next single, *From A Rabbit*, knocked some of the stuffing out of Radio Stars. Sessions for their sophomore album were vanishing into a morass of fussy arrangements and clever-clever lyrics. The group's traditional drumming problems resurfaced as Parry quit and his replacement, the New Hearts' Jamie Crompton, became embroiled in a dispute with his former manager. And Chiswick itself began to look unstable.

A second guitarist, Trevor White (also ex-Sparks, and the producer of *Dirty Pictures*) was recruited, but the band's trials continued. Scheduling problems ensured that SONGS FOR SWINGING LOVERS would not hit the stores until November 1978, weeks after the Radio Stars' latest tour wrapped up, by which time Martin Gordon, at least, was heartily sick of the entire affair. He quit in December 1978. Jamie Crompton followed. And while Ellison, Mcleod, White and a returning Steve Parry did continue on for a while, demoing a third album and playing some remarkably ramshackle shows through the summer of 1979, they finally gave up in July.

The Gordon / Ellison axis would reform in 1982 for a string of live shows and one new single, *My Mother Said*, released on Gordon's own Snat label (there would also be a compilation, 2 MINUTES MR. SMITH.) A decade later, Ellison and White resumed their own variation on the group for occasional live shows to coincide with the release of the compilation SOMEWHERE THERE'S A PLACE FOR US. Somewhere, there was.

RADIO STARS DISCOGRAPHY

Singles
- *Dirty Pictures / Sail Away* (Chiswick S9, 1977)
- STOP IT! EP (Chiswick SW17, 1977)
- *Dirty Pictures / Horrible Breath* (Chiswick NS23, 1977)
- *From A Rabbit / To A Beast* (Chiswick NS36, 1978)
- *Radio Stars / Accountancy Blues* (Chiswick CHIS 104, 1978)
- *Real Me / Good Personality* (Chiswick CHIS 109, 1979)
- *Good Personality / Talkin' 'Bout You* (Moonlight MNS 001, 1982)
- *My Mother Said / Two Minutes Mr. Smith* (Snat ECG 001, 1982)

Albums
- SONGS FOR SWINGING LOVERS (Chiswick WIK 5, 1977)
- HOLIDAY ALBUM (Chiswick CWK 3001, 1978)
- TWO MINUTES MR. SMITH (Moonlight MNA 001, 1982)
- SOMEWHERE THERE'S A PLACE FOR US (Chiswick CDWIK 107, 1992)

≪ 26 ≫
Tom Robinson Band

"Only a bitter and twisted personality could actively dislike the Tom Robinson Band," the New Musical Express once remarked and, over the course of the group's first four singles at least, there were few folks who'd disagree. Born, the band's own publicity claimed, as "a red-blooded reaction against the growing number of reactionary rock buffoons," TRB emerged early in 1977 with a string of powerhouse gigs around London's sweatiest (and, in the main, least punk-influenced) venues and instantly proved themselves capable of becoming the most successful of all Britain's most blatantly political groups. Ever.

Glad To Be Gay, I'm Alright Jack and, best of all, *Power In The Darkness*, all took murderously accurate swipes at the country's greatest evils — racial and sexual discrimination — but in such a manner that even the crassest slogan (and Robinson wrote enough of them) was effective.

Robinson himself first came to note as a member of early-mid 70's folk rockers Café Society. Signed to Ray Davies' Konk concern, they were best known for the volume of their grumbles against their label, frustrations that led the group to break up in mid-1976.

Robinson and drummer Mick Trevisick promptly formed the Tom Robinson Band with a starting line-up of guitarist Anton Mauve, bassist Mark Griffiths and guitarist Bret Sinclair. "I had several songs ready. During the latter days of Café Society I had written *Martin*, *Grey Cortina*, *Glad To Be Gay*, *Long Hot Summer* . . . and just as I was leaving, I wrote *2-4-6-8 Motorway* and not long after that, *Up Against The Wall*. Then I filled out with cover versions which seemed to be in the direction I wanted — *Waiting For The Man* and *I Shall be Released*."

This line up made its debut at the Hope & Anchor on November 28, 1976, then broke up immediately after. Over the next few months, Robinson constructed an entire new line-up, featuring guitar hero Danny Kustow, Mark Ambler (keyboards) and Brian "Dolphin" Taylor (drums.)

The group's live appeal was unmistakable, their popularity unbelievable. But for six months, attempts to land a record deal appeared doomed to failure. Both Stiff and Virgin rejected the group outright and, while Jet were interested for a time, they were ultimately scared off by Robinson's increasingly volatile gay stance. Only EMI were truly interested, and in July, the match was made official. The label requested just one concession — that TRB introduce themselves to the record buying public with one of the few non-controversial songs in their repertoire, the pounding, driving anthem *2-4-6-8 Motorway*.

TRB complied and were rewarded with a Top 5 hit which, naturally, was seen by many of the group's earliest supporters as a complete cop out. But, of course, it made sound commercial sense, in the long term as much as the short. Although the music press had been flying Robinson's political and sexual preferences high for most of the year, both the singer and EMI were well aware that the news would have to reach the general public before the group's message could be set free in the marketplace. And that's how it worked. With the gutter press playing on the gay angle, touting Robinson as David Bowie's butch brother and ramming his *Glad To Be Gay* badge down every throat which opened the paper, and TRB furiously playing every venue they could get in the wake of the hit, by early 1978 the stage was set for the live RISING FREE EP.

Produced by Chris Thomas, fresh from his stint with The Sex Pistols, the EP replaced a projected (and still unreleased) studio version of *Glad To Be Gay* in the group's schedule, and the biting rendition which opened RISING FREE was ample proof of why. Even though it was another track, *Don't Take No For An Answer,* which received the most airplay, there was little doubt which song became the hit that spring.

RISING FREE reached No. 18, and TRB was now headlining across the country. It didn't matter what lured the kiddies in, once they were there they had no alternative but to listen. *Up Against The Wall,* the group's third single, was released in May, rising to a lowly No. 33, but balancing that was the Top 5 success of POWER IN THE DARKNESS, the group's debut album.

A slavering slab of bitterness and anger, it was without doubt the most successful album of all the year's "political" offerings. It touched upon all of Robinson's pet subjects, from his laddish yearning for a gray Cortina to the "Only Lovers Left Alive" doomsday scenarios of *Winter Of 79* and *You Gotta Survive,* and on to the title track, an unremarkable rent-a-rocker which suddenly, and with painstaking deliberation, exploded into a poisonous translation of a right wing political broadcast, Chris Thomas' crystal clear production bringing every last word slamming out of the mix.

Thomas himself doesn't rate the album too highly. "It probably wasn't the right decision to make that album, although I got on well with the band ... I was enjoying it, but definitely in retrospect it all started sliding downhill. Tom lost interest in the album while he was away in the States doing interviews, and the writer wasn't there to consult, so it became a little bit hard." His reservations do not impact on the album.

Throughout 1978-79, TRB could be found almost everywhere. They became regulars at Rock Against Racism shows, including the greatest of them all, at Alexander Palace. There, Robinson stood on the very brink of everything he had strived towards — consummate showman, influential rhetorician, and political superstar. But attempts to record a second album at Rockfield, again with Chris Thomas producing, were finally abandoned after a month of wasted studio time and it was suddenly apparent that the group's appeal was slipping.

"It's only by looking at the press, or the TV documentary (filmed by Granada TV in late 1978) that you remember just how big we were," Robinson mused later. Suddenly, audiences seemed less enthusiastic, ticket sales were slowing, the group itself was having difficulty translating new material to the same heights as the old. New songs that premiered as the group continued the round of touring seemed dull, barely inspired rewrites of the first set's proudest moments. There was nothing to threaten *Glad To Be Gay,* nothing to outsell *Motorway.*

Ambler quit; so did his replacement, Roogalator's Nick Plytas. Dolphin, too, departed. Robinson and Kustow ended up going into the studio with two virtual strangers, drummer Preston Heyman and keyboardist Ian Parker.

TRB 2 was finally produced by Todd Rundgren — and the media massacred it. Rundgren himself admits, "Working with [them] was great, but putting up with the critical fall-out afterwards was horrible. Doing the album was just a lot of fun for everyone, but what happened makes you think. You get in the studio and record a record as quickly as we did — which was a little over a week, and everybody has such a good time making it that you think, 'Great, this must be a step in some direction'. Then to have it completely slagged off to the point that the record company runs away with its tail between its legs and refuses to promote the record, it really makes you wonder sometimes."

It made Robinson wonder, too. The July 1980, departure of Kustow was the final straw. Announcing he was "in no mood to carry on a Tom Robinson Band without any of the Tom Robinson Band in it," Robinson recorded one final TRB single with a session group, *Never Gonna Fall In Love Again* (co-written with Elton John), then announced the end of the group.

The final word on the group was the hits collection TRB 3, sensibly built around a dozen non-LP songs. Played alongside POWER IN THE DARKNESS, it justifies every great thing ever written about TRB — justifies them and proves them.

Early in 1978, Julie Burchill and Tony Parsons decided, "[TRB] are the first band not to shrug off their political stance as soon as they walk out of the recording studio. The first band with sufficient pure, undiluted, unrepentant bottle to keep their crooning necks firmly on the uncompromising line of commitment when life would be infinitely easier — and no less of a commercial success — if they made their excuses and left before the riot. Compared to the Tom Robinson Band, every other rock musician is wanking into the wind."

TOM ROBINSON BAND DISCOGRAPHY

UK Singles
- *2-4-6-8 Motorway / I Shall Be Released* (EMI 2715, 1977)
- RISING FREE EP: *Don't Take No For An Answer / Glad To Be Gay / Martin / Right On Sister* (EMI 2749, 1978)
- *Up Against The Wall / I'm Alright Jack* (EMI 2787, 1978)
- *Too Good To Be True / Power In The Darkness* (EMI 2847, 1978)
- *Bully For You / Our People* (EMI 2916, 1979)
- *All Right All Night / Black Angel* [unreleased] (EMI 2946, 1979)
- *Never Gonna Fall In Love / Getting Tighter* (EMI 2967, 1979)

US Singles
- *2-4-6-8 Motorway / I Shall Be Released* (Harvest 4533, 1977)
- *Right On Sister / Glad To Be Gay* (Harvest 4568, 1978)
- *Bully For You / Our People* (Harvest 4726, 1979)

UK Albums
- POWER IN THE DARKNESS (EMI 3226, 1978)
- TRB 2 (EMI 3296, 1979)
- TRB 3 (compilation) (EMI EMC 1005, 1981)

US Albums
- POWER IN THE DARKNESS (Harvest 11778, 1978)
- TRB 2 (Harvest 1930, 1979)

≪ 27 ≫
The Stranglers

Formed in the leafy southern English village of Chiddington in 1974, The Guildford Stranglers were the classic example of a group being in the right place at the right time. With the group itself deeply divided musically between a pub-rock take on keyboard ridden prog and a flaming infatuation with the Doors, only bassist Hugh Cornwell had any real credentials at the time — his schoolboy group, Emil & The Detectives, had featured future Fairport Convention mainstay Richard Thompson. For the others, though, it was just one loser group after another — all apart from Jean Jacques Burnel, who had done little more than give classical guitar lessons to local children.

By their own admission, The Guildford Stranglers were a terrible group, plowing around the countryside churning out a chain of bass and organ heavy dirges which rarely assaulted the same venue twice. Even after they made it up to London in late 1975, having shortened their name to The Stranglers in an attempt to camouflage their suburban origins, they found the going heavy. But with the pub rock scene already in its death throes, promoters were willing to book anything new, simply to give the regular punters a break. And so The Stranglers opened for anyone they could and, slowly, experience combined with stubborn persistence and saw them begin to attract a partisan following.

The stirrings of punk had an immediate effect on the band, musically, but more important, socially. The Strangler's best songs were the confrontational ones, pleasantly titled ditties like *Peasant In The Big Shitty, I Feel Like A Wog, Down In The Sewer, Ugly* — sensing, even in the early days, the growth of a movement which appeared, at least superficially, to glorify precisely the same cultural failings as the group themselves were fixated by, they threw themselves into the ring.

Yet they were never to become "insiders" — a late night club brawl with The Sex Pistols saw to that. By that time, however, The Stranglers had already achieved an honor which no other British group could have dreamed of, opening for The Ramones on their July 4, 1976 London debut — to a review-reading audience that was still trying to fit a sound to this punk rock business which the papers were full of, The Stranglers fit in by association alone.

Mark P, editor of the newly launched punk fanzine Sniffin' Glue, too, was converted. "Their sound is 1976 . . . The Stranglers are a pleasure to boogie to — sometimes they sound like The Doors, other times like Television, but they've got an ID of their own."

In October, The Stranglers opened for another visiting New York icon, Patti Smith. Poor sound and the audience's impatience ensured they cleared the auditorium long before they'd completed their set, but by the time the band set out on their first UK tour, the UA label had signed them. Once the gigging was over, the recording could begin.

Whatever the true nature of The Stranglers' relationship to punk in early 1977 — lawless, outcast soul brothers or misogynist fat ugly uncles — there was, as John Peel put it, a compelling seediness to their music, a quality which producer Martin Rushent immediately brought to the fore. The Stranglers' debut single, (Get A) Grip (On Yourself) should have been just another rent-a-rant about the rigors of playing Rock and Roll for a living — instead, it developed into a dark, mysterious mumble, underpinned by a sinister backing

track which left one in no doubt that something awfully portentous was happening.

RATTUS NORVEGICUS, their debut album, echoed that and then some — conceived as a straightforward recounting of the band's live set, bolstered by some suitably subterranean sound effects, it emerged a compulsive trawl through the darker recesses of the punk (and worse!) psyche, an outspoken litany of all the evils and traumas which polite society imagined flourished within the heart of this wicked new musical fad.

Neither were The Stranglers averse to taking a stand to match their music. Against all of UA's better instincts, the group insisted on releasing the sexually explosive Peaches as their second single, conceding only that the utterly inoffensive Go Buddy Go could be added as a double A-side. They were rewarded with a top 20 hit.

On stage, too, the band welcomed opprobrium. Cornwall had recently taken to wearing a T-shirt which cunningly redesigned the Ford logo to read "fuck." Now, as the group prepared to play London's Roundhouse, the local council warned that the T-shirt was banned from the premises. Cornwall wore it regardless, concealed beneath another shirt for much of the show, but then revealing it for the encores. No matter that he took it off almost immediately — a ban had been breached, the power was cut and the group faced (but ultimately avoided) a ban from ever again appearing within the capital's boundaries.

Another crisis loomed when the French authorities announced that, with two French parents, Burnel was eligible — and, indeed, wanted — for military service. He, too, escaped, but the band's good fortune could not continue forever. The first dates of their next UK tour were cancelled after Cornwall collapsed with flu. More were lost after rioting at a Clash gig in London provoked a fresh round of Punk Rock Rampage Horror stories. When the tour did finally get going, Burnel was beaten up in Cleethorpes after suggesting that the audience stop fighting one another and try it on with him. More violence forced the cancellation of the group's Swedish tour.

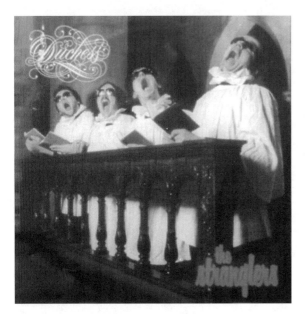

Amidst all this action, a return to roots gig at the Nashville in London saw the band joined onstage by Celia Gollin, a singer their manager had "discovered" at a Chelsea restaurant. The set that night included a terrific version of *Mony Mony* and, in June, vinyl evidence of The Stranglers' ability to stay in the same room as a female without sending her screaming into the streets came when they disguised themselves as The Mutations and backed Celia on that same song. (A second Celia single, *You Better Believe Me*, followed in November.)

Something Better Change, the Stranglers' third hit single, was released in July 1977, an exciting prelude to NO MORE HEROES, The Stranglers' second album (the title track became their fourth single.) That, of course, was a huge hit, but a gross disappointment. The Stranglers' first album had already cherrypicked the best bits from the group's long-established live set (well, most of them anyway.) The second, recorded in a hurry, simply picked up the loose ends, lackluster versions of the already out-dated *I Feel Like A Wog*, *Bring On The Nubiles* and *Peasant In The Big Shitty*.

Hastily the band retrenched, issuing a quickfire brace of new singles, *Five Minutes* and *Nice'n'Sleazy*, a song which did much to encapsulate the group's image (and, typically, make a joke of its harsher elements.) Another new album not far behind it — BLACK AND WHITE was highlighted not only by *Nice'n'Sleazy*, but was also by a retelling of the band's experiences in Sweden (dedicated to the local Raggere right wing bully boys), plus a behemothic recounting of the pop classic *Walk On By*, slowed to murderously mogadon proportions and reduced to an emotional grindstone.

More importantly, however, BLACK AND WHITE proved that The Stranglers were no longer reliant on either shock or shame for their best ideas — that, behind the gruff, sexist exteriors there beat hearts of . . . well, not gold, but not pure evil, either. Indeed, the live album, X CERT, which followed would put a cap on that entire phase of The Stranglers' existence — henceforth, their output would brighten with their outlook.

1979's THE RAVEN was positively chirpy in places and, though they continued over the next few years to broach dark and sometimes dangerous subjects (*Golden Brown*, a surprisingly acoustic 1982 hit single, extolled the virtues of heroin), by the time of their first hits collection, again in 1982, it was stunning to see just how many "classic" "pop" singles The Stranglers had unleashed.

Through the 1980's The Stranglers kept going, dicing with the psychedelic revival which threatened to break through much of that benighted decade, and surfacing, too, to further pollute the Top 20 with the sweet *Skin Deep*, and covers of the Kinks' *All Day And All Of The Night* and Question Mark & the Mysterians' *96 Tears*.

They survived the 1990 departure of Cornwall — he was replaced by former Vibrator John Ellis. They overcame, too, the temporary loss of Jet Black. A keen appreciation of their history, meanwhile, kept the group kicking even harder as they okayed releases for their earliest demos and live recordings, BBC session material and, in 1992, a lavishly packaged boxed-set. Even more impressively, they retained something of their old menace as well. As Cornwall himself once remarked, when questioned about The Stranglers' longevity (their third album had just been released), "The thing with The Stranglers is, we want to become established. It's the establishment we have problems with."

THE STRANGLERS DISCOGRAPHY
UK Singles 1977-79
- *Grip / London Lady* (UA UP 36211, 1977)
- *Choosey Susie / Peasant In The Big Shitty* (UA FREE 3, 1977)
- *Peaches / Go Buddy Go* (UA UP 36248, 1977)
- *Something Better Change / Straighten Out* (UA UP 36277, 1977)
- *No More Heroes / In The Shadows* (UA UP 36300, 1977)
- *Five Minutes / Rok It To The Moon* (UA UP 36350, 1978)
- *Nice'n'Sleazy / Shut Up* (UA UP 36379, 1978)
- *Sverige* (Swedish language) / (UA UP 26459, 1978)
- *Walk On By / Tits / Mean To Me* (UA FREE 9, 1979)
- *Walk On By / Tank / Old Codger* (UA UP 36429, 1978)
- *Duchess / Fools Rush Out* (UA BP 308, 1979)
- *Nuclear Device / Yellowcake UF6* (UA BP 318, 1979)
- *Don't Bring Harry / Wired / Crabs / In The Shadows* (UA STR 1, 1979)

US Singles 1977-79
- *Something Better Change / Straighten Out / Grip / Hangin' Around* (A&M, 1977)

UK Albums
- IV RATTUS NORVEGICUS (UA UAG 30045, 1977)
- NO MORE HEROES (UA UAG 30200, 1977)
- BLACK AND WHITE (UA UAG 30222, 1978)

○ LIVE — X CERTIFICATE (UA UAG 30224, 1979)
○ THE RAVEN (UA UAG 30262, 1979)
○ THE COLLECTION 1977-82 (Liberty LBG 30353, 1982)
○ RARITIES (Liberty EMS 1306, 1988)
○ THE SINGLES (EMI CD1314, 1989)
○ WINTER OF DISCONTENT (compilation including *Something Better Change*)
  (Strange Fruit SFRCD 204, 1990)
○ THE EARLY YEARS: RARE LIVE AND UNRELEASED (New Speak SPEAK 101, 1992)
○ LIVE AT THE HOPE & ANCHOR 1977 (EMI 7987892, 1992)
○ THE OLD TESTAMENT (boxed-set) (EMI CDSTRANG 1, 1993)

US Albums
○ IV RATTUS NORVEGICUS (A&M 4648, 1977)
○ NO MORE HEROES (A&M 4659, 1977)
○ BLACK AND WHITE (A&M 4706, 1978)
○ LIVE — X CERTIFICATE (IRS 70011, 1979)

≪ 28 ≫
The Table

Where monsters dwell, where creatures roam ... With an opening line like that, *Do The Standing Still* was always destined to become one of the most distinctive singles of 1977, to promise one of the most distinctive careers, and produce one of the most distinctive mysteries. Who were The Table, where were they from and — perhaps more importantly — what were they on?

Do The Standing Still appeared with no fanfare whatsoever in April 1977, ostensibly introducing a new dance, but in reality fashioning a cataclysm of sound which was simply irresistible.

The band themselves were Welsh, forming in Cardiff in 1971 under the singularly odd name of John Stabber, around a nucleus of two professional cartoonists, Russell Young (vocals, space-age guitar, keyboards and bass) and Tony Barnes (vocals, Martian guitar, and bass.) The pair gigged in general obscurity for much of the early 1970's, although they did make it onto the 1974 Windsor festival bill, borrowing equipment from another of the featured groups for the occasion. Throughout their career, both as John Stabber and later, the band prided itself upon owning no gear of their own.

Augmented by Mickey O'Connor (mystery guitar) and Len Lewis (drums), the group re-emerged as Do You Want A Table in 1976. They gigged sporadically, secretly, but seldom less than spectacularly. In concert, the (now abbreviated) Table were bathed in brilliant onstage cartoon graphics; following the release of the single, audiences, hitherto leaping around with gay, period abandon, would pay their own tribute to the song by indeed standing still throughout its performance.

Incredibly well-received, *Do The Standing Still* prompted the NME to interview The Table. The journalist came away with little more than the dire threat of an album whose highlights would include the recitation of a shopping list. But the album never materialized and, aside from a couple of appearances on punky compilations (both GUILLOTINE and CATCH A WAVE featured reprises of *Do The Standing Still*), The Table themselves stood still for the next 14 months.

Then, without warning, Barnes, Young and new guitarist Kevin Bannon re-emerged with *Sex Cells*, an infuriatingly brief but again irresistible 45, nailed into place by a chorus which insisted, "I'm obsessed with a mad desire for sex with schoolgirls." Understandably, it did not get much airplay and The Table never bothered following it up. The group vanished off the face of the earth. Barnes and Young presumably went back to cartooning. A mere four tracks are all that remains to prove they ever even existed. But what a great four tracks they were.

THE TABLE DISCOGRAPHY
Singles
- ○ *Do The Standing Still / Magical Melon Of The Tropics* (Virgin VS 176, 1977)
- ○ *Sex Cells / The Road Of Lyfe* (Chiswick NS 31, 1978)

⋖ Part Four ⋗
– They Came, They Saw . . . –

⋖ 29 ⋗
Big In Japan

Liverpool's finest hour. Born out of the excitement of The Clash gig there on May 5, 1977, Big In Japan was the brainchild of future KLF mainstay Bill Drummond, a man born to coax night-time psychedelics from his tortured guitar, Ian Broudie (guitar — later, founder of the Lightning Seeds), former Deaf School guitarist Clive Langer (one day, one half of 80's production dream team Langer-Winstanley), vocalist Jayne Casey — the screeching mass of day-glo hair who would go on to front the inimitable Pink Military, bassist Kevin Ward and drummer Phil Allen.

Dominating the local scene, harbingers of a new Merseyboom which would, in time, spawn Teardrop Explodes, Echo And The Bunnymen, Orchestral Manouvres In The Dark, Wah, Dead Or Alive and so many more, Big In Japan were a fixture at Eric's, the city's best known punk club. Indeed, when it came time to cut their first single, *Big In Japan*, it was Eric's own eponymous label which would release it. (The B-side, by the Chuddy Nuddies, disguised the identity of the 'pool's only other band of note at that time, the Yachts.)

Seldom performing outside of their own environment, Big In Japan powered through 1977 with barely a care in the world. As the year drew to a close, however, so did the spirit of raucous naivety which had prompted the group to form in the first place. Out went founder members Kevin Ward and Phil Allen. In came a desire to become the hottest thing on Merseyside and, by Christmas, it was a very different group which threatened to see in the new year.

A new bassist, Ambrose Reynolds, came in and then went out again — he was succeeded by a 17 year old former Judy Garland clone named William Johnson, known to all as Holly ever since a girlfriend compared him to Warhol superstar Holly Woodlawn. Drummer (and future Slit / Banshee) Budgie was recruited from the underachieving Spitfire Boys, and Casey shaved her head and took to performing with electrodes taped to her skull.

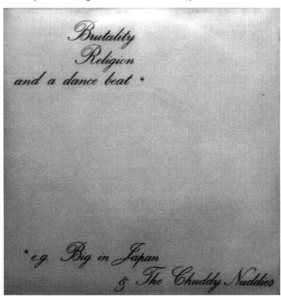

It was Johnson's first group, although he denied he was completely inexperienced. "I have served my apprenticeship. I started writing songs at 13 in our front room." By 16 he had progressed to manhandling Jacques Brel's *My Death* in front of club audiences, a boy, his acoustic guitar and, he admits, a stage full of flying glass. Despite such credentials, he was thrown in at the deepest end the band could conceive, at their London debut on November 28, 1978, and acquitted himself with bow-tie wearing dignity.

He was not, however, to be Big In Japan for long. In June 1978, after no more than six months, Johnson quit, announcing that, with a little help from Ian Broudie, he was going solo. Undeterred, Big In Japan marched towards their second single, the superlative FROM Y TO Z AND NEVER AGAIN EP. Before it could be released, however, the members took a momentous decision — they split, bidding farewell at Eric's (where else?) on August 26. The EP duly appeared in November, debuting Drummond's newly-formed Zoo Records — at which point, a skeleton Big In Japan resurfaced, around Casey, Broudie, Johnson and Budgie.

This line up squeaked out a third single and revisited London for a March 1979, Peel session, before breaking up for the last time. One member, however, would go onto become Big In Japan and everywhere else — Holly Johnson linked with another ex-Spitfire Boy, Paul Rutherford, and formed Frankie Goes To Hollywood.

BIG IN JAPAN DISCOGRAPHY
Singles
- *Big In Japan* / Chuddy Nuddies cut (Erics 001, 1977)
- FROM Y TO Z AND NEVER AGAIN EP: *Nothing Special / Cindi And The Barbi Dolls / Suicide A Go Go / Taxi* (Zoo CAGE 01, 1978)
- *Kizza Me / Dream Lover* (Aura AUS 103, 1979)

≺ **30** ≻
Blunt Instrument

Blunt Instrument formed in London in May 1977. Drummer David Sinclair had recently moved to London from his home in Giffnock, Scotland, and remembers, "I was the only person who turned up to an audition conducted by [guitarist / vocalist] Robert Sandall and [bassist] Ed Shaw. The other member, Bill Benfield [guitar] wasn't there either. I only met him at the first rehearsal. At the time, they didn't even have a name, so it could fairly be said that I was in at the beginning."

It was the age of instant gratification, a time when punk groups could form, gig and split up all in the space of a day — it is indeed a sobering thought that both The Buzzcocks and The Damned have now existed far longer in their reunited states than they ever did in the original form.

For Blunt Instrument to march from the rehearsal room to the stage within a week of coming together, then, was nothing unusual. Neither was the speed with which they rushed out their debut single, the thunderous *No Excuse*. And neither was the success that awaited it. *No Excuse* soared to No. 2 on that most fondly remembered precursor of today's British Independent chart, a New Wave listing administered by Lightning Records, and published weekly in the Sounds music paper.

Blunt Instrument had the world at their feet, it seemed. Their name alone was enough for the tabloid newspaper The Sun to include them in a shock horror A-Z of Punk, rubbing shoulders with the established nasties of the genre, and that despite the band adamantly eschewing all but the most basic links to punk rock. They played the same venues as the rest of the pack, but that was it. Rather, Blunt Instrument looked back to an earlier age, when it was still legal to say you liked the Stones, and Johnny Rotten was simply a colloquial name for a decaying condom (this is true. It was.)

Such yearnings didn't dent the group's popularity, nor the punkish megaton exuberance of their audience. Indeed, Blunt Instrument had a full two months worth of shows already lined up when Sinclair, having been struck on the head by a flying cider bottle, fell off his drum stool at a Kings Cross street party and fractured his wrist.

That was on July 29, 1978. It would be fall before the band was working again, by which time they had undergone at least two major changes. They changed their guitarist, then they changed their name.

Benfield quit almost before Sinclair was out of the emergency room. A teacher by profession, he had only ever regarded Blunt Instrument as a part time outfit, and Sinclair recalls, "the last I heard of him, he was in Tokyo, teaching English. But he was a masterful blues guitarist, even if he never got much chance to show it in the Blunts."

He was replaced by Nick Aldridge. Sinclair's wrist was still in plaster at the audition, but the excitement in the room was tangible all the same. It was like a fresh start, and that meant coming up with a fresh name. They chose London Zoo because everyone had heard of it, and were promptly assailed by a host of witty quips relating to the real Zoo. "Big in Regents' Park" was the most popular, although it swiftly turned out that the group was going to be bigger in Scotland.

Early in 1979, London Zoo signed to that most enterprising of period indies, the Edinburgh based Zoom Records, home to the infant Simple Minds, and another band-that-should-have-done-better, the Zones (formed, incidentally, from the Midge Ure-less ashes of teenybop idols Slik.) *Receiving End* (backed with the self-mythologizingly titled *London Zoo*) the group's debut single, was a jangling burst of staccato exhilaration, comparable to Television's *Marquee Moon* in places, and characterized by a stunning rhythm guitar break in the middle.

By the spring of 1980, London Zoo had composed over fifty songs, but it was unlikely that they'd ever get the chance to do anything with them. Dropped by Zoom after the label was absorbed into Arista, London Zoo recorded and pressed the *Who's Driving This Car* 45 themselves, releasing it on their own, deliberately misspelt Gramaphone label. But a few airings from John Peel and fellow BBC DJ Mike Read were the extent of the group's acclaim. They played their final (113th) show on May 22, 1980 at the Swan pub in Hammersmith, then went their separate ways.

Sinclair went on to ex-Advert TV Smith's Explorers, but never forgot his past — filling in one of those Favorite Color/Record/Hairstyle-type questionnaires for the Explorers' fanzine a year or so after London Zoo's demise, under "Greatest Disappointment," Sinclair wrote simply, "the failure of London Zoo to achieve commercial success."

BLUNT INSTRUMENT DISCOGRAPHY
Singles
  ○ *No Excuse / Interrogation* (Diesel DCL 01, 1978)

LONDON ZOO DISCOGRAPHY
Singles
  ○ *Receiving End / London Zoo* (Zoom ZUM 12, 1980)
  ○ *Who's Driving This Car / You And Your Big Ideas* (Gramaphone STB 80, 1980)

⪡ 31 ⪢
Boomtown Rats

Through the mid-1970's and the musical wasteland which separated the first flowering of glam rock from the initial shockwaves of the Pistols and Co., the term "punk rock" had little meaning, but a great deal of currency.

Bruce Springsteen, briefly, was termed a punk, as was Nils Lofgren and, with at least a little historical resonance, the emergent Patti Smith (sans Group.) In the UK, both Thin Lizzy and Graham Parker touched similar nerves. Indeed, anybody capable of wearing a leather jacket with a modicum of street-smart style, and composing lyrics that matched the look, was fair game for this new archetyping and, in dispassionate terms, there was some accuracy to it. The very word "punk," after all, comes loaded with meaning — wiry, snot-nosed upstarts sauntering through the gangster / youth landscapes of vintage Hollywood, from Brando and Dean to the Dead End Kids. It only stood to reason that punk rock should apply to the same set of values.

A genre in search of progenitors, "punk" never sat comfortably on the shoulders it was placed upon. Sure, Springsteen and Lofgren (and Patti) had attitude galore, and the right kind of subject matter, too. But they also had conventions and a kind of heartland morality which left nobody in doubt that at the end of the day, the hero would get the girl, the bad guy would see the error of his ways, and everyone would drive off happy together, in a big pink Chevy with the radio on.

And punks couldn't afford Chevys.

Neither could the Boomtown Rats, but from home base Dublin, Bob Geldof, Johnny Fingers, Garry Roberts, Gerry Cott, Pete Briquette and Simon Crowe eyed the emergent scene across the water in England. And eyed, too, the distinctly home-grown Springsteeny element which made the best of Geldof's songs so great, and knew that if the two could somehow be put together . . .

Signing with the Ensign label, a clutch of shows around London through summer 1977 paved the way for the Rats' breakthrough. Landing the opening slot on Tom Petty's first London headline shows, the Irish band graffiti'd London with a simple message — "Rats Eat Heartbreakers." And on stage, they came close to doing so.

Three solid singles were machine gunned into play over the next six months — *Looking After #1*, *Mary Of The 4th Form* and *She's So Modern*. But it was when you stepped inside the Rats' eponymous debut album that their true precedents screamed loudest, a straight line which moved from the Stones to Thin Lizzy — *Joey*, the most obviously indebted of the Ratmeister's efforts, the Stonesy-ballady *You Can Make It If You Try*, and the jerked agitpunk of *Neon Heart*. Across the entire record, the Rats' game plan was revealed in all its sparkling glory.

What nobody expected was an ambition to match. Riding the brilliantly quirk-laden TONIC FOR THE TROOPS sophomore album, their fourth single, *Like Clockwork*, was an audacious, ambitious tour de force, a new wave classic before the tide had even turned in that direction. Had it turkeyed, the Rats might well have retreated back to basics. When it succeeded, they were ready to reveal all.

The stark street classic *Rat Trap* was a merciless snapshot of UK '78, a litany of social decay. Springsteen's *Jungle Land* hung around similar street corners, as did Patti's The Boy Looked At Johnny, and Lizzy's *The Boys Are Back In Town*. But *Rat Trap* nailed a zeitgeist which those others could barely spell, the mind-numbing torture of adolescence in agony — having to turn up TOP OF THE POPS to drown out the sound of mum and dad fighting, kebab houses with cheap formica tabletops, mindless, directionless boredom every night. It soared to No. 1 and it seemed, in musical terms, that punk could go no further. In creative terms, however, the Rats intended ensuring that it did.

Inspired, but more accurately, emboldened, Geldof's next move — his piece de resistance — was his most devastating yet, *I Don't Like Mondays*. Another No. 1, the saga of an American schoolgirl who went on a shooting rampage at school, ensured the Rats' superstardom and would, naturally, begin spelling out their downfall. Geldof had, by all reasonable expectations, peaked. But reason is in short supply when the media — musical and otherwise — is proclaiming you a genius and waiting for the next masterpiece to pour from the pen.

Boomtown Rats

The Rats' third album, THE FINE ART OF SURFACING, was excellent. Its accompanying singles — the paranoia paradise of *Someone's Looking At You*, the suicide blonde of *Diamond Smiles* — spellbinding. But over all, *Mondays* hung like a predatory bat, defying Geldof to top it and ensuring, by its very presence, that he never would. SURFACING was followed by the declining values of both MONDO BONGO and V DEEP and, though the Rats could still turn out classic singles when they had to (the deliciously post-ska *House On Fire*, the Spectoresque *Never In A Million Years*), the end was both messy and inevitable.

In 1984-85, as the Rats awaited the release of a final album (IN THE LONG GRASS) which even they knew was doomed, Geldof masterminded the Band Aid / Live Aid spectaculars. The Rats played their last ever show at the latter, before Geldof launched a sporadic solo career — sporadic, of course, because he has since ascended to the ranks of household-name celebrity without really having to do much of anything. Bruce Springsteen, on the other, just keeps going . . . and going . . . and going.

BOOMTOWN RATS DISCOGRAPHY
UK Singles

- *Looking After #1 / Born To Burn / Barefootin'* (Ensign ENY 4, 1977)
- *Mary Of The 4th Form / Do The Rat* (Ensign ENY 9, 1977)
- *She's So Modern / Lying Again* (Ensign ENY 13, 1978)
- *Like Clockwork / How Do You Do?* (Ensign ENY 14, 1978)
- *Rat Trap / So Strange* (Ensign ENY 16, 1978)
- *I Don't Like Mondays /* (Ensign ENY 30, 1979)
- *Diamond Smiles / Late Last Night* (Ensign ENY 33, 1979)
- *Dun Laoghaire* (flexi) (Flexipop 003, 1979)
- *Someone's Looking At You / When The Night Comes* (Ensign ENY 34, 1980)
- *Banana Republic / Man At The Top* (Ensign BONGO 1, 1980)
- *Elephant's Graveyard / Real Different* (Ensign BONGO 2, 1981)
- *Never In A Million Years / Don't Talk To Me* (Mercury MER 87, 1981)
- *House On Fire / Europe Looked Ugly* (Mercury MER 91, 1982)
- *House On Fire / dub / Europe Looked Ugly* (12") (Mercury MER 91, 1982)
- *Charmed Lives / No Hiding Place* (Mercury MER 106, 1982)
- *Charmed Lives / No Hiding Place / Nothing Happened Today / Storm Breaks* (doublepack) (Mercury MER 106, 1982)
- *Charmed Lives / No Hiding Place / A Storm Breaks* (12") (Mercury MERX 106, 1982)
- *Tonight / Precious Time* (Mercury MER 154, 1984)
- *Tonight / Precious Time / Walking Downtown* (12") (Mercury MERX 154, 1984)
- *Drag Me Down / Icicle In The Sun* (Mercury MER 163, 1984)
- *Drag Me Down / Icicle In The Sun / Rat Trap / She's So Modern* (12") (Mercury MERX 163, 1984)
- *Dave / Hard Times* (Mercury MER 179, 1984)
- *Dave / Hard Times / I Don't Like Mondays / It's All The Rage* (doublepack) (Mercury MER 179, 1984)
- *Dave / Hard Times / Banana Republic* (live) / *Close As You'll Ever Be* (live) (12") (Mercury MERX 179, 1984)
- *A Hold On Me / Never In A Million Years* (Mercury 184, 1985)

US Singles
- *I Don't Like Mondays / It's All The Rage* (Columbia 11117, 1980)
- *Someone's Looking At You / I Don't Like Mondays* (Columbia 11248, 1980)
- *Up All Night / Another Piece Of Red* (Columbia 60512, 1981)
- *Charmed Lives / Never In A Million Years* (Columbia 03386, 1982)
- *Icicle In The Sun / Rain* (Columbia 04892, 1985)
- *Drag Me Down / Hard Times* (Columbia 05590, 1985)

UK Albums
- BOOMTOWN RATS (Ensign ENVY 1, 1977)
- TONIC FOR THE TROOPS (Ensign ENVY 3, 1978)
- FINE ART OF SURFACING (Ensign ENROX 11, 1979)
- MONDO BONGO (Mercury 6359 082, 1981)
- V DEEP (Mercury 6359 082, 1982)
- IN THE LONG GRASS (Mercury MERL 38, 1984)
- GREATEST HITS (compilation) (Mercury, 1989)

US Albums
- BOOMTOWN RATS (Mercury SRM 1188, 1978)
- TONIC FOR THE TROOPS (Columbia 35750, 1978)
- THE FINE ART OF SURFACING (Columbia 36248, 1979)
- MONDO BONGO (Columbia 37062, 1980)
- V DEEP (Columbia 7150 082, 1982)
- IN THE LONG GRASS (Columbia 39335, 1984)

⋖ 32 ⋗
The Flys

In 1976, Dave Freeman, Joe Hughes and Neil O'Connor, together with a string of unnamed drummers, were the Coventry based Midnight Circus, becoming The Flys after Pete King, brother of the band's manager, joined up. An introduction to The Damned (musically) and The Buzzcocks (personally) gave the group a fairly regular opening slot for the latter group and, in April 1977, The Flys' first demos went out.

The response was less than deafening — spring 1977, after all, was a time when everybody was so busy looking for the Next Big Thing that no-one actually had time to listen for it and, by early winter, the somewhat disgusted Flys were readying a five track EP for self-release.

Half punk, half pop, a jangling, jarring cross between The Byrds and The Buzzcocks, A BUNCH OF FIVE appeared just in time for Christmas, 1977 — at which point, EMI finally offered The Flys a deal. Weeks later, the band was in London, opening for labelmates The

Rich Kids at the 100 Club (they blew the headliners off stage) and preparing for their first single, a major label release for the EP's *Love And A Molotov Cocktail* — the first undisputed classic 45 of 1978.

Springtime tours with The Buzzcocks and the magnificence madness of Otway-Barrett followed, together with a new single, *Fun City*. Summer then saw The Flys record their debut album, WAIKIKI BEACH REFUGEES — a power punk tour de force, its title track alone worth the price of entry. A dramatic reworking of *Fun City*, together with *Saturday Sunrise* and *Looking For New Hearts*, furthered their credentials.

The Flys were now headlining their own shows, albeit still confined to the club circuit, but with sufficient sway to organize their own support acts. One of their more inspired choices was Neil O'Connor's sister Hazel, a would-be singer with a nice line in Lene Lovich impersonations. It was chance alone which decreed that sundry associates of would-be movie mogul Dodi Al Fayed should be at the Marquee that particular night. Hazel was scooped off to fame, fortune and a role in the post-punk apocalypse movie BREAKING GLASS. Her brother's group just carried on scraping round the clubs.

Released in gorgeous banana colored vinyl, the single of *Waikiki Beach Refugees* came close to giving the Flys a hit — but not close enough. *Beverly* and *Name Dropping* followed it into the bunker and slowly, cruel fate began pulling the legs off The Flys.

Pete King was replaced by Graham Deakin (ex-John Entwistle's Ox) shortly before work began on the group's second album, FLYS' OWN (King resurfaced in After The Fire and also played with Electric Light Orchestra. Sadly, he died of cancer aged 26.) The Flys, meanwhile, buzzed through a competent, but none too dramatic new album, highlighted by *Energy Boy* and *Fascinate Me*, but never once approaching the exquisite heights of *Molotov Cocktail* or *Waikiki Beach*. Indeed, if there was any unifying feature to the record, it was the gloomy sound of a band crumbling around the edges, the sharpness of earlier work dulled by repeated disappointment.

Live they were still capable of holding their own, as they proved when they toured with The Ruts in the fall of 1979. But *We Are The Lucky Ones*, the utterly inappropriately titled new single, failed. An EP, FOUR FROM MANCHESTER SQUARE and another single died, and EMI's patience was at an end. For two years, label and group alike had marched along convinced that one more single, one more gig, was all it would take for a breakthrough. It was time to call a halt to it all.

The Flys were finally swatted in early 1980, never reforming but at least enjoying a revival in their fortunes in the early 1990's with the release of a well-received compilation. Neil O'Connor, meanwhile, made a dramatic appearance on Die Toten Hosen's version of *Molotov Cocktail* (from their LEARNING ENGLISH punk tribute album.)

THE FLYS DISCOGRAPHY

Singles
- BUNCH OF FIVES EP (Zama ZA 10, 1977)
- *Love And A Molotov Cocktail / Can I Crash Here? / Civilization* (EMI 2747, 1978)
- *Fun City / EC4* (EMI 2795, 1978)
- *Waikiki Beach Refugees / We Don't Mind The Rave* (EMI 2867, 1978)
- *Beverly / Don't Moonlight On Me* (EMI 2907, 1979)
- *Name Dropping /* (EMI 2936, 1979)
- *We Are The Lucky Ones / Living In The Sticks* (EMI 2979, 1980)
- FOUR FROM MANCHESTER SQUARE EP (Parlophone R6030, 1980)
- *What Will Mother Say? / Undercover Agent Zero* (Parlophone R6036, 1980)

Albums
- WAIKIKI BEACH REFUGEES (EMI EMC 3249, 1978)
- FLYS OWN (EMI EMC 3316, 1980)
- THE FLYS (See For Miles, 1991)

⋘ 33 ⋙
London

London was formed in late 1976 by Miles Tredinnick, a former assistant to impresario Robert Stigwood. Running a couple of ads in the music press and renaming himself Riff Regan (in honor of his favorite characters from WEST SIDE STORY and the British police drama THE SWEENEY), he knew precisely what he was looking for — musicians loose enough to play punk at its most raucous and uncompromising, but tight enough not to mess it up.

Drummer Jon Moss, bassist Steve Voice and guitarist Colin Wight (who promptly changed his name to Dave Wight . . . ah, those outrageous punks!) answered his summons, and with a few weeks of manic rehearsal under their belt, the band debuted at the Rochester Castle, a pub in Stoke Newington, north London.

It was a fairy tale from the beginning. Amongst the curious crowd gathered at the venue that night was one Danny Morgan, assistant to legendary manager Simon Napier Bell. By the end of the week, Napier Bell was London's manager, touting them around town as the most charismatic group he'd seen since the vintage Rolling Stones.

By the new year, London was headlining their own club shows, and heading on the road for three months with The Stranglers, themselves riding high with their *Grip* debut single. It was a tough initiation, marred throughout by the growing national backlash to All Things Punk. Ever since The Sex Pistols' infamous appearance on prime time television, punk had become a pariah in many provincial towns, with local councils canceling shows at a moment's notice, and on a moment's whim. The Stranglers / London outing suffered as much as any other, but still the experience paid off. In March 1977, London signed to MCA Records and were despatched to record their debut single.

Produced by Napier Bell, the triumphant *Everyone's A Winner* was issued in May and immediately things started happening. A video was shot under the watchful eye of acclaimed television director Mike Mansfield. A wealth of encouraging reviews were more than matched by sales, And with the group gigging regularly through the spring and summer, MCA was convinced they had a hit act on their hands. They were wrong.

London's second single followed in August. Leading off with the knowing *Summer Of Love*, it served up no less than three B-sides: the blistered *No Time*; a paean to Regan's favorite punk pin-up *Siouxsie Sue*; and a fabulous cover of the Easybeats' *Friday On My Mind*, based on David Bowie's PIN UPS version, but imbibed with a delicious punk pout. It was a great record, fabulous value for the money, and again, London looked set for a hit.

Indeed, *Summer Of Love* climbed to No. 52 on some charts and, one week that fall, London was so close to an appearance on TOP OF THE POPS that they could almost taste the backstage sandwiches. Only one thing stood in their way, the possibility that there was maybe a rude word or two lurking somewhere within *Summer Of Love*. There wasn't, but still the BBC insisted on having a set of handwritten lyrics couriered over to the studios . . . and all for nothing. Mid-week sales had dropped off dramatically and the magic call never came. Instead, London consoled themselves with the knowledge that, when one of the newspapers cornered Heather McCartney, daughter of Beatle Paul, to ask her what she thought of this punk rock business (everyone knew, after all, what punk rock thought of her dad), she admitted she liked it . . . and London were one of her favorites.

November 1977 brought the group's third single, *Animal Games*, an appearance on the late night rock television show SO IT GOES, and the promise of a full length album early in the new year. That, too, was titled ANIMAL GAMES, arriving in a gloriously tacky cover featuring a giant, Kong-like gorilla demolishing a drum kit and its occupant with it — and how appropriate was that. Turning in his most dramatic production work since his days with 60's psychedelic mavericks John's Children, Napier Bell coaxed sheer mayhem out of the band. Unfortunately, even as London came of age, they ran out of time.

On October 1, 1977, The Damned were shaken by the departure of founder member Rat Scabies and, having first auditioned what guitarist Brian James remembers as "fifty useless drummers," the group finally asked Jon Moss to replace him. He agreed.

Moss played his last ever gig with London at the London Marquee, just before Christmas 1977, and, though Regan left the stage promising "we'll see you next year," a string of rehearsals failed to turn up a single suitable replacement for Moss. Early in the new year, London agreed to break up. Ironically, The Damned followed suit shortly after and Moss went off to try his luck elsewhere, working alongside a flamboyant London scenester named Boy George in a brand new concept called Culture Club. Apparently they did quite well for themselves.

LONDON DISCOGRAPHY

UK Singles
- *Everyone's A Winner / Handcuffed* (MCA 305, 1977)
- *No Time / Siouxsie Sue / Summer Of Love / Friday On My Mind* (MCA 319, 1977)
- *Animal Games / Us Kids Cold* (MCA 336, 1977)

UK Album
- ANIMAL GAMES (MCA MCF 2823, 1978)

≺ 34 ≻
The Nipple Erectors

The intoxicated success of Shane MacGowan's Pogues, a success which took them from the spit'n'sawdust environment of north London's Irish pubs to the top of the British chart, to the set of SATURDAY NIGHT LIVE, to the threshold of Something Really Big, surely ranked among the 1980's most unusual tales. And one of its most delayed.

A full decade before Pogue Mahone came staggering out of the pub, at least one member of the group, singer MacGowan, had also seemed poised for big things. That he didn't attain them then might well have been a blessing, sensitive latterday Pogues fans still cringed when reminded that the group's original name, Pogue Mo Chone, translated from Gaelic as "Kiss My Arse." Imagine those same poor souls having to admit their favorite band was the Nipple Erectors.

Shanne Bradley played a raucous bass and had Damned-to-be Captain Sensible for a music teacher. Guitarist Roger was ex of an early incarnation of punky hopefuls The Tools. Another guitarist, Adrian Thrills, was better known as an NME journalist. And Shane "O'Hooligan" MacGowan, as everyone knew, was the Face of '76. At least, that's what the headline swore when his picture appeared on the cover of Sounds, before he'd even dreamed up the Nipple Erectors, and it might even have been true. Everyone, after all, had seen the famous photograph of O'Hooligan at The Clash's ICA gig, blood pouring from a bite to the earlobe. Everyone had heard about the night he got so carried away by a Jam show that he ended up breaking their speakers. Now he hoped that everybody would hear of The Nipple Erectors, because with a name like that, it would be hard to avoid them.

The group's name was a test of punk morality. The punks failed. Not only did The Nipple Erectors find it hard to get gigs with a moniker like that, they also found it hard to get people to come to the precious few gigs they did land. Yet, if their supporters could be counted on the fingers of one hand, they were influential names regardless: Sounds resident genius journalist Jane Suck, Adrian Thrills (of course), and the owners of the Rock On record store in Soho Market all lined up to praise the Nipple Erectors, with

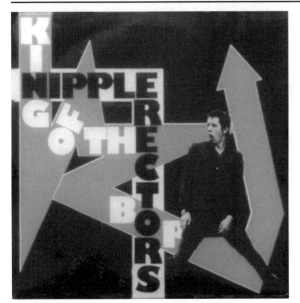

the latter even forming their own record label, Soho, specifically to unleash the band on a wider audience. In early 1978, with no other record company showing even a token interest in the group, Rock On sat through the Nipple Erectors' demo, *My Degeneration*, then promptly handed them a recording contract.

The first ever release on Soho, *King Of The Bop* was a remarkably coherent representation of everything the Nipples were about. The band's attentions had long been heading into rockabilly country (it was the media which rechristened it punkabilly — primarily, admitted Bradley, "because we couldn't play it very well"), and when *King Of The Bop* was kindly received, The Nipple Erectors returned to the studio to work on their follow-up.

A lot had changed in the interim, though. The surname-less Roger was gone, off selling postcards in the National Gallery. Their latest drummer, Gerry, too, had left and, for a short time he could be found in an archaic incarnation of The Pretenders. It was even rumored that Shanne Bradley had gone, but in reality she'd simply changed her name to Dragonella to stop people confusing her with O'Hooligan.

On guitar now was Larry Hindricks, best known for his impromptu performance as Damned vocalist one night when Dave Vanian forgot to turn up. He'd been taught to play by Mark Harrison from hard rocker Bernie Torme's group and, one night six months later, when the Nipples positively destroyed the dimming Damned on stage at the Hope & Anchor, who should be standing in on drums but ... Mark Harrison. Ex-Eater drummer Phil Rowlands sat in for a while as well. Indeed, sticksmen came and went like nobody's business, so the band basically ignored the chaos at the back and just got on with their next single, the R&B tinged *All The Time In The World*.

Fresh ambition accompanied the release. Suddenly tiring of having people tell them that, were it not for the group's name, they could be positively enormous, the Erectors became the nicely inoffensive Nips and, having replaced Hindricks with someone named Fritz, they set to work on their masterpiece, *Gabrielle*. At least, everyone else said it was a masterpiece. O'Hooligan, on the other hand, called it "a silly pop record" and admitted, "I am fucking ashamed to be associated with it. All these bands nowadays are making 'good' pop records, and I fucking hate 'good' pop records. It just doesn't mean anything in 1980, or it shouldn't, anyway."

The thing with punk, MacGowan continued, "was that nobody knew what the fuck was going on. I got into the turgid basement of punk in its bad days. I was snorting sulphate, spending money on drinks which were over-expensive and missing the groups I was supposed to be watching. It was a load of crap in the end. The only bands I ever really liked were the original four: the Pistols, The Clash, The Jam and especially, The Damned. They summed up the true punk attitude. The only ones I've liked since then are The Members and Sham 69."

Not that shame prevented him from carrying on. The months on either side of *Gabrielle* saw the group turn up supporting The Jam, Dexy's Midnight Runners, arch modsters Purple Hearts and the quaintly squeaky Dolly Mixtures. Paul Weller even talked of producing them, although when a Nips' album did finally appear, Weller was as far away from it as anyone. ONLY AT THE END OF THE BEGINNING was a prophetic title anyway. Despite one final single, *Happy Song*, appearing close to a year after *Gabrielle*, the Nips were dead. And when they finally admitted it, in late 1981, hardly anybody even noticed. They were too busy wondering what Pogue Mo Chone could possibly mean . . .

THE NIPPLE ERECTORS DISCOGRAPHY
UK Singles
- *King Of The Bop / Nervous Wreck* (Soho SH 1, 1978)
- *All The Time In The World / Private Eyes* (Soho SH 4, 1978)
- *Gabrielle / Vengeance* (Soho SH 9, 1980)
- *Happy Song / Nobody To Love* (Test Press 5, 1980)

UK Albums
- ONLY AT THE END OF THE BEGINNING (Soho HOHO 1, 1980)
- BOPS, BABES, BOOZE & BOVVER (Big Beat WIK66, 1987)

⋘ 35 ⋙
The Rezillos

Edinburgh, Scotland art students Eugene Reynolds and Jo Callis formed the Rezillos in early 1976 around a mutual love of science fiction, 60's pop culture and, initially, the same sense of theatrical outrage then firing the likes of Deaf School and Ian Dury's Kilburn And The High Roads.

Taking their name from a comic book, REZILO CAFÉ, it was only as time passed and new sounds filtered into earshot that The Rezillos' sound toughened up, by which time the band's ranks had swollen to include vocalist Fay Fife, Mark Harris (guitar), Dr. DK Smythe (bass) and Angel Paterson (drums), in which form the group thrashed their way onto the Scottish circuit, a gorgeously garish explosion of high pop camp, low-brow kitsch and a taste for the same kind of knowing trash nostalgia which would later make a star of HI

FIDELITY / LIKE A BOY author Nick Hornby. Forgotten candy bars, half-remembered records and TV shows, all the detritus of disposable society found a home in The Rezillos' sonic landfills and, so long as you knew what they were on about, they were utterly irresistible.

In spring 1977, local entrepreneur Lawrie Love signed the group to his Sensible label. They repaid his patronage with what would become one of the undisputed classic single of the year, the mighty *Can't Stand My Baby*. A group whose name had barely been mentioned south of the border was suddenly on everybody's lips and, within weeks, The Rezillos were signing to Sire.

Smythe and Patterson left to be replaced by the immaculately named William Mysterious and The Rezillos' major label debut, *(My Baby Does) Good Sculptures* appeared in November, another well-received opus which amplified the band's growing penchant for quirk-ridden punkarama pop.

Culture vultures supreme, the group began seriously messing with their audience's preconceptions. One still remembers the expressions of pained horror which came over

audience's faces as the band ran through the showstopping *"Someone's Gonna Get Their Head Kicked In Tonight*, then informed the pogoing masses that it was an old Fleetwood Mac cover. The riff to Deep Purple's *Smoke On The Water* was another favorite — Fife later recalled how delightful it was to see a room full of sweaty punks go crazy for a song which they'd profess to abhor with the passion of lovers.

It was with summer 1978's TOP OF THE POPS that The Rezillos finally broke through in a big way, storming the Top 20 (and the TOTP studios) even as their debut album, DESTINATION VENUS, rocketed chartwards. Another triumphant single, the album's title track, followed, but behind the scenes, all was not well. Mysterious left, to be replaced by the saintly Simon Templar. Barely a month later, however, the newcomer followed Callis and Paterson into a new group, Shake.

Stunned by the defections, Fife and Reynolds wrapped up The Rezillos with one further single, *Cold Wars*, and a valedictory live album, the very appropriately titled MISSION ACCOMPLISHED . . . BUT THE BEAT GOES ON. They then reconvened as The Revillos, reiterating many of The Rezillos' cultural reference points, but with an even more pronounced Americana retro bias — comparisons with The B-52s would not be too far off the mark.

THE REZILLOS DISCOGRAPHY
Singles
  ○ *Can't Stand My Baby* / *I Wanna Be Your Man* (Sensible FAB 1, 1977)
  ○ *Flying Saucer Attack* / *Good Sculptures* (Sire 6078 612, 1977)
  ○ *Cold Wars* / *William Mysterious Overture* (Sire 6198, 1978)
  ○ *Top Of The Pops* / *20,000 Rezillos . . .* (Sire 4001, 1978)
  ○ *Destination Venus* / *Mystery Action* (Sire 4008, 1978)
  ○ *Cold Wars* / *Flying Saucer Attack* / *Twist And Shout* (Sire 4014, 1979)

Albums
  ○ CAN'T STAND THE REZILLOS (Sire K56530, 1978)
  ○ MISSION ACCOMPLISHED (live) (Sire SRK 6069, 1979)

⋖ 36 ⋗
Rikki And The Last Days Of Earth

"My name's Rikki Sylvan . . ." announces — you guessed it — Rikki Sylvan, as the opening instrumental of his debut album shatters to its conclusion . . . "and these are The Last Days Of Earth." And we still don't know whether he was referring to his band, who were indeed called The Last Days Of Earth, or to some unimagined apocalypse which he was convinced was about to befall us. But listening through what swiftly established itself amongst the most powerful albums of 1977-78, it's not hard to guess which one he thought he meant. The world was about to fall apart, and Rikki Sylvan was here to orchestrate armageddon.

From the beginning, conventional wisdom insisted, they were doomed. Chris Spedding was a great role model if you wanted to be a leather-dripping sideman, and who could possibly forget his starring role in Bryan Ferry's latest group? But this entire group looked a bit like Spedding, which made Sylvan's obvious vocal debt to Ferry seem even more ironic.

What really marked Rikki And The Last Days Of Earth down for death-by-1000-bad-reviews, however, was their music. Now, let us not mistake world-weary disappointment for some kind of condemnation — FOUR MINUTE WARNING, the band's one and only album, is uniformly wonderful. But only if your own musical tastes take the same turning away from primal Diamond Doggerel as fueled the Doctors Of Madness and powered the original Ultravox, the same turn, of course, that Robert Fripp would eventually be taking on EXPOSURE, which David Bowie would seek out on LODGER, and which Gary Numan would develop into a minimalistic artform before the decade was over.

In 1978, however, all that was about as fashionable as the Twist. Like the Doctors, like Ultravox, Rikki And The Last Days Of Earth had caught a glimpse of the future. It wasn't their fault it was wearing David Bowie's old science fiction trousers.

The first stirrings of these last days were unleashed across a late 1977 single, City Of The Damned / Victimized. Both tracks summed up Sylvan's crippled vision of decadence, darkness, destruction — a bleak / oblique vision of a world without hope which nevertheless believed the whole shebang would hold together long enough for the group to get its album out. And that was both its, and the album's, downfall. Whereas other contemporary doom-mongers, even the Doctors at their most maggoty pessimistic, couched their dire predictions in understatement and (comparative) subtlety, Sylvan painted his in mile high neon.

There was nothing unequivocal about it. City Of The Damned, Outcast, Aleister Crowley, Twilight Jack, Victimized, Sylvan's world was one of unrelenting psychopathology, a cult of demented loners who straddled society stratas like a chainsaw wielding colossus. Even Loaded, the album's one concession to humor (and second single), set the listener's teeth on edge as Sylvan played the role of the ultimate Nouveau Rich kid — and prophesied 80's yuppiedom with way too much accuracy. A clutch of sweeping instrumentals — the opening For The Last Days, the sibilant No Wave, the tumultuous Four Minute Warning — unified these same disparate themes. "Imagine Roxy Music's Out Of The Blue played by the Hitler Youth Marching Band," marveled one critic, and then, playing on the title of sundry ambient Eno albums, he retitled it "Music For Berlin Bunkers."

In May 1978, DJM released what would become Rikki's final single, Twilight Jack. Like its predecessors, like the album, it flopped abysmally and when the history of the new wave finally started to get written, Rikki And The Last Days Of Earth were conspicuous by their absence — no-one remembered, nobody cared.

But if they'd actually listened, how different things might have been.

RIKKI AND THE LAST DAYS OF EARTH DISCOGRAPHY
UK Singles
  ○ *City Of The Damned / Victimized* (DJM DJS 10814, 1977)
  ○ *Loaded / Street Fighting Man* (DJM DJS 10822, 1978)
  ○ *Twilight Jack / No Wave* (DJM DJS 10860, 1978)

UK Album
  ○ FOUR MINUTE WARNING (DJM, 1978)

◄ 37 ►
The Ruts

Over the course of 18 months, from the fall of 1978 until the death of vocalist Malcolm Owen on July 14, 1980, The Ruts established themselves as perhaps the most compelling group on the British punk scene. Politically aware, but rarely sloganeering, The Ruts stood at the crossroads of punk, reggae and oi!, and gave their heart to all three. The fact that they accomplished it all with just one official album, and a handful of singles, only emphasizes their power. If The Ruts had survived into the 1980's, the 1980's as we know them would probably never have happened.

The band members — Owen, guitarist Paul Fox, drummer Dave Ruffy and bassist John Jennings — were west London school friends before they were bandmates, and The Ruts' initial efforts concentrated upon their immediate neighborhood. The group's first ever live show came as support for Wayne County's Electric Chairs at High Wycombe Town Hall in mid 1978. Their most regular gig was the White Hart in Acton. Just another provincial group, with provincial gigs in provincial pubs. And then they offered their services to the nascent Rock Against Racism.

The late 1970's were a period of racial turmoil in London, particularly in the suburbs which The Ruts called home, where the fascist National Front party battled for supremacy (or perhaps, sheer bloody-mindedness) with the area's immigrant population. Rock Against Racism knew that a handful of rock bands, playing together under a catchy banner was never going to change that. But they might influence the people who could and, over the next couple of years, RAR became a potent force in British politics. The Ruts would remain a key mover in that potency.

The group's first RAR gigs saw them sharing the bill with Misty In Roots, a Southall based reggae band. It was an inspired coupling which not only showcased the two groups' musical abilities, it also sharpened their appreciation of one anothers' work. Other white English bands had dipped into the reggae songbook to varying degrees of success. The Ruts were the first (The Clash and The Police notwithstanding) to make that songbook their own and, by the end of 1978, The Ruts were ready for the studio, in all their hybrid glory.

In A Rut, backed by the anti-heroin anthem *H Eyes*, offered little indication of the group's musical strength. A fairly straightforward punk anthem, it was nevertheless a strong live favorite and its release on Misty In Roots' own People Unite label quickly established The Ruts on the independent chart.

They carried the commitment and the energy of the early Clash, before that band surrendered to the psycho-babble of FM-oriented conscientious rabble rousing. They mixed rock concerns with reggae influences. And they were catchy as hell. Even so, Virgin, who signed The Ruts in the spring of 1979, were as surprised as anyone when the group sealed the deal with a hit. *Babylon's Burning* rammed The Ruts into the Top 10. A tour with The Damned saw the follow-up, *Something That I Said*, keep them in the Top 30. And, in October, The Ruts released their debut album, THE CRACK.

What an album it was. From the police siren which opens side one, wailing into *Babylon's Burning*, through the sub-punk thrashing of *Out Of Order* and *Human Punk*, and onto the stunning *SUS*, THE CRACK remains the last crucial album of the 70's, with its closing track, *Jah Wars*, the last crucial single.

The culmination of The Ruts' dub punk hybrid, *Jah Wars* was written following the April 23, 1979 race riots which shook the predominantly black Southall neighborhood, a battle which culminated with one death, 300 arrests and countless injuries. Released just as the first rioters went to trial, there wasn't a radio station in the land courageous enough to actually play the song, but that wasn't the point. *Jah Wars* confirmed The Ruts' ascendancy all the same.

The group's first headline tour followed, while a visit to France saw national television serve up a major documentary on them. In 1980 a new single, *Staring At The Rude Boys*, acknowledged the 2-Tone / ska revival then swirling around the punk underground and climbed to No. 22. The Ruts had the world at their feet. Their second album beckoned, and so did America. Another British tour early in the year reinforced the feeling that The Ruts were about to become the band of the new decade.

Of course, it wasn't to be. Before The Ruts extinguished the need, Malcolm Owen had been drowning his personal sorrows with smack, and freely acknowledged the autobiographical content of *H Eyes*. The break-up of his marriage, early in the new year, brought many of those sorrows back into cruel focus and, by the time The Ruts' latest tour reached the southwestern town of Plymouth, the singer was in a bad way. The gig was cancelled. So was the next one, and the one after that. Almost overnight, the remainder of the tour had been wiped out.

It was crisis time, but Owen seemed willing to work towards recovery. While the rest of The Ruts took to the studio to begin planning the next album, Owen retired to convalesce. It seemed to do the trick as well. That spring, he rejoined the group in the studio, to record a new single, *West One*. But he was still using, and on July 14, a massive overdose let the world in on his secret.

The Ruts story did not, of course, end there. *West One* faltered at No. 43 on the chart, but while Owen's stricken bandmates regrouped as Ruts DC (for Da Capo: "new beginning"), skewering direction and abandoning success in favor of an even deeper pursuit of reggae and dub, Virgin Records, no strangers to posthumous plundering (as the Sid Vicious catalog reminds us), hastily cobbled together what would become the second Ruts album, the out-takes and B-sides collection GRIN AND BEAR IT.

THE RUTS DISCOGRAPHY
UK Singles
- *In A Rut / H-Eyes* (People Unite RUT 1A, 1979)
- *Babylon's Burning / Society* (Virgin VS 271, 1979)
- *Something That I Said / Give Youth A Chance* (Virgin VS 285, 1979)
- *Jah War / I Ain't Sofisticated* (Virgin VS 298, 1979)
- *Rude Boys / Love In Vain* (Virgin VS 327, 1980)
- *West One / The Crack* (Virgin VS 370, 1980)
- *Babylon's Burning / Something That I Said / Rude Boys / West One* (Virgin VS58312, 1983)
- THE PEEL SESSION EP (1921979): *Sus / Society / You're Just A . . . / It Was Cold / Something That I Said* (Strange Fruit SFRPS 011, 1987)

UK Albums
- THE CRACK (Virgin V2132, 1979)
- GRIN AND BEAR IT (compilation) (Virgin V2188, 1980)
- LIVE (Dojo LP52, 1987)
- LIVE AND LOUD (Link 013, 1989)
- THE PEEL SESSIONS (Strange Fruit SFRCD 109, 1990)
- BBC RADIO ONE IN CONCERT (Windsong WIN 009, 1991)

≪ **38** ≫
The Shapes

The Shapes were a mystery from the beginning. Though popular local legend insists that they'd been thrashing around Leamington Spa since 1977, when diminutive vocalist Seymour Bybuss and bassist Brian Helicopter played their first ever show — miming to *At The Hop*, with Bybuss wearing a gorilla mask. It would be another year or so, however, before the group recruited drummer Dave Gee and guitarists Tim Jee and Steve Richards, by which time The Shapes' one hope of stardom had, apparently, already passed them by.

An earlier line-up had been invited to provide the entertainment at a party in nearby Stratford Upon Avon, a town singled out by tour guides as William Shakespeare's birthplace, but one which was also occasionally visited by DJ John Peel. He attended this party, caught The Shapes in full flight, then departed, "secure in the knowledge that I would never see or hear the little beasts again."

The Shapes, however, were not so easily put off, and in February 1979, the band booked themselves a few hours in the local Woodbine Studios, allegedly from the proceeds of Helicopter selling his goldfish — although like so much else in The Shapes' story, this could just be apocryphal nonsense. Whatever the truth behind the group's finances, they emerged with four songs which they sensibly decided to incorporate onto one 7-inch disc, the aptly titled PART OF THE FURNITURE EP — aptly titled, that is, because they'd already decided to form a record label called Sofa.

It opened with the deliciously plaintive *Wot's For Lunch Mum (Not Beans Again)*, possibly modeled upon one listen too many to the Who's psychedelic masterpiece *Heinz Baked Beans*. Or not. Another masterpiece recounted a sighting of *Batman In The Launderette* (Holy Soap!) . . . it was irresistible stuff and, by the time a copy of the EP found its way to John Peel, he had so overcame his earlier distaste that he happily agreed to play it . . . then play it and play it and play it again. By the time the record's shelf life was over, A PART OF THE FURNITURE had sold over 10,000 copies, and hit No. 2 on the indy singles chart.

Throughout the spring of 1979, The Shapes gigged constantly, opening for The Cure, The Saints, The Fall and more, none of whom at that point in time were much bigger than The Shapes themselves. They did some more recording, laying down the definitive version of *Leamington*, and the first of The Shapes' trilogy of science fiction masterpieces, the close encounters of the quirky pop kind-esque *Alien Love*.

They applied themselves to the serious business of publicity too, by having their photographs taken wearing large, cardboard, geometric boxes on their heads — half moons, triangles, circles, squares and stars, "shapes," of course. And they entered into serious negotiation with the first record company to pay them any attention whatsoever.

Shortly after their first JOHN PEEL broadcast, The Shapes were contacted by Terri Hooley, the Belfast based mastermind behind the Good Vibrations label, home to John Peel's other favorite band, The Undertones. A distribution deal was struck, whereby Sofa and Good Vibrations would pool their resources for a joint release, and the following day, The Shapes were back in the studio, hammering down versions of the gleefully macabre *Airline Disaster* and a seemingly impromptu noise fest called *Blast Off!*.

Released as a double B-side, and with the Good Vibrations marketing machine cranking into maximum overdrive, *Airline Disaster* not only sold less copies than its year old predecessor, it allegedly sold less than just about any other record released that year — a consequence, in those safety conscious days, of writing a plaintive ("airline disaster oooh-oooh, I think we're going to crash") ode to falling out of the sky. And not even a happy ending to the disaster itself was going to alter that.

Airline Disaster* would later earn the accolade of becoming the first Shapes song to make it onto CD, when it was included on a Good Vibrations label retrospective in the early 1990's. At the time, though, the single's failure presaged nothing but bad luck for the group. Guitarist Richards quit only weeks after the single sunk out of sight, and after one more frenetic burst of live work, the band decided to concentrate on studio work, and another joint Sofa / Good Vibrations release.

Unfortunately, finances — or the lack thereof — intervened, and with them, further dislocation within The Shapes themselves. Matters finally came to a head as the group came out on stage at the London Marquee, when Bybuss' attempt to leap on stage and grab the microphone completely backfired — he missed the mike, missed the stage, and ended up introducing stage diving to an audience which simply didn't know what to do with him. So, they passed him over their heads, across the dance floor, past the bar, and out of the door. And all the while, the group kept playing, even after it became apparent that Bybuss would not (for whatever reasons) be rejoining them, not that night . . . not ever.

THE SHAPES DISCOGRAPHY
UK Singles
  ○ PART OF THE FURNITURE EP (Sofa 1, 1979)
  ○ *Airline Disaster / Blast Off* (Sofa 2, 1980)

UK Album
○ SONGS FOR SENSIBLE PEOPLE (Overground OVER 81, 1998)

◄ 39 ►
U.K. Subs

The story of the U.K. Subs is the story of persistence, stubbornness, and a dogged refusal to bow down to any outside pressure whatsoever. Throughout their 23+ year existence, the band has been reviled, ignored, dismissed and all but destroyed. But they have kept right on going regardless, still gigging, still recording, still espousing a spirit which is older than their audience and meaning every last word of it.

They have had hits and they survived. They've been feted as stars and never succumbed. And they've undergone so many line-up changes that even singer and sole surviving founder Charlie Harper probably can't remember every past member. But as long as he remains constant, the Subs will go on. As long as he remains constant, the rest is irrelevant.

The U.K. Subs launched during the summer of 1977 when Harper's then current group, the Marauders, changed their name to the Subs, then changed it again to avoid conflicts with a Scottish band of the same designation. The change didn't do much to the group's sound — caught live in London during early 1977, the Subs still pursued a hopped-up pub rock hybrid not too dissimilar to the kind of pub rock-inflected sounds The Vibrators had been making six months earlier.

The October, 1977, arrival of guitarist Nicky Garratt marked the dawn of the true Subs age — out went most of the material which the band (Harper, bassist Paul Slack and drummer Steve Jones (no relation to the ex-Pistol) had hitherto been playing. Out, too, went most of their own personal tastes in music. Garratt was punk through and through, a hard riffing Stooges / Dolls / Pistols freak who slammed those same sounds into the Subs.

The Shapes

By the end of the year, the Subs were regulars at the recently reborn / still-born Roxy Club and, when the venue finally gave up the ghost with a dodgy live album, FAREWELL TO THE ROXY, the Subs were far and away the best thing in sight, slamming through the anthemic *I Live In A Car* and *Telephone Numbers*. The Subs also appeared at the Liverpool leg of the Stiff / Chiswick Challenge, a traveling talent contest aimed at finding suitable new talent for the two independent labels. They didn't win (the evening's triumph belonged to The Smirks), but they didn't really need to.

Drummer Jones quit. So did his replacement, Rory Lyons. In May, with Pete Davies now in the hot seat, the Subs recorded their first dramatic JOHN PEEL session. Weeks later, the independent City Records label picked them up for an EP.

Almost unnoticed and certainly unremarked upon by the UK music press, the Subs' live support was growing fast. Fermenting the discontent many kids were feeling about the direction in which punk was moving, the haste with which the biggest groups had already (early 1978) embraced mainstream tastes and preferences, the ease with which the cold fire of the movement's early promise had been extinguished by new tastes and tastefulness, the Subs' incendiary live show took its lead from the early Sex Pistols — controlled chaos (with the emphasis decidedly not on the word "controlled"), executed in front of an audience that gave as good as it got.

Harper himself was the ultimate frontman, snapping turtle furious, hurtling around the stage like a demon possessed, pebbledashing lyrics which could have been T-shirts or tattoos, so deeply ingrained in the audience did they become. The Subs EP shot to the top of the independent chart without the overground observers even knowing it existed. By the time the majors did finally catch on to the Subs' appeal, they'd already missed the boat. The band signed with GEM Records, slammed out *Stranglehold* in May 1978, and hit the Top 30 without breaking a sweat.

The Subs toured (Julian Temple, architect of the Pistols GREAT ROCK'N'ROLL SWINDLE, filmed the affair for the PUNK CAN TAKE IT mini flick), then returned to the studio to cut their debut album, the ferocious ANOTHER KIND OF BLUES — 17 tracks of unrelenting pure punk.

A new single, *Tomorrow's Girls*, kept the Subs in the Top 30. An unlikely cover of the Zombies' *She's Not There*, successful not only because it was a great song, but also

because the Subs resisted the temptation to do a Dickies on it, followed. The group toured the US, opening for The Police; hit Europe with The Ramones in early 1980 . . . for the next couple of years at least, the routine of tour / hit single / new album was to become almost grinding, kept fresh only by the freshness of the band itself.

The Subs' second album, BRAND NEW AGE, served up more of the expected. Their third, the dramatic live CRASH COURSE, likewise. Oi! had broken out across the punk scene, and the Subs were its elder statesmen, a tangible link with the punk of the past and the promise of the future — if early admirers umm-ed and aah-ed a little now, when the prospect of going to see the group arose, that, too, was a sign of the band's warp-speed development and pace.

CRASH COURSE, of course, was simply a stopgap, a consolidation of the story so far. With new bassist Alvin Gibbs hauled out of the wreckage of Brian James' Hellions, and drummer Steve Roberts in replace, the Subs bounced back into action with October 1980's *Party In Paris*, excerpted from the DIMINISHED RESPONSIBILITY album, and the madness intensified.

Departing for Cyanide, then for Beki Bondage's so cruelly underestimated Ligotage, Roberts would be replaced by ex-Chelsea / Gen X / Adverts drummer John Towe in November 1981 — Towe himself had most recently been working with former Bay City Roller Ian Mitchell's La Rox, and had changed his name to Kim Wylie for the occasion. For whatever reason, he retained the pseudonym into the Subs, wearing it across their fifth album, ENDANGERED SPECIES, in October 1982.

The title was apt. By the end of the year, Wylie / Towe had gone again and the U.K. Subs themselves had shattered. Garratt formed a new group, Rebekka Frame, and Gibbs and Harper became the Urban Dogs — the singer had already sampled a solo career, during a break in Subs action back in 1980. It did little and the Dogs were to do no more. By the summer of 1983, he had reunited with founder bassist Slack and was piecing together a new U.K. Subs.

The new band, naturally, picked up where the old had left off — neither their schedule had changed, nor their outlook. For half of the 1980's and most of the 1990's, the Subs existed and that was all you needed to know (although modern ears may care that Rancid's Lars Frederickson was a member for a while.) 1998, however, brought them back to full bloom, headlining the trans-America Social Chaos tour, with a line-up reinvigorated by Garratt and Gibbs, and a set which hit all the right notes without once looking over its shoulder at the good old days. At a time when even the era's most deified groups had proved unable to resist that opportunity, the importance of the U.K. Subs just hit home even harder.

U.K. SUBS CLASSIC YEARS DISCOGRAPHY 1978-82
Singles
- *CID / I Live In A Car / BIC* (City NIK 5, 1978)
- *Stranglehold / World War / Rockers* (GEM 5, 1979)
- *Tomorrow's Girls / Scum Of The Heart / Telephone Numbers* (GEM 10, 1979)
- *She's Not There / Kicks / Victim / The Same Thing* (GEM 14, 1979)
- *Warhead / Waiting For The Man / The Harper* (GEM 23, 1980)
- *Teenage / Left For Dead / NY State Police* (GEM 30, 1980)
- *Party In Paris / Fall Of The Empire* (GEM 42, 1980)
- *Keep On Running / Perfect Girl* (GEM 45, 1981)
- *Countdown / Plan Of Action* (NEMS NES 304, 1981)
- *Shake Up The City / Police State / Self Destruct / War Of The Roses* (Abstract 012, 1982)

Albums
- ANOTHER KIND OF BLUES (GEM 100, 1979)
- BRAND NEW AGE (GEM 106, 1980)
- CRASH COURSE (GEM 111, 1980)
- DIMINISHED RESPONSIBILITY (GEM 112, 1981)
- ENDANGERED SPECIES (Abstract, 1982)
- PUNK ROCK RARITIES (Captain Oi AHOY 93, 1998)

≪ **40** ≫
Vice Squad

Asked to describe herself for her fan club's fanzine in 1984, Beki Bondage had no hesitation. "Beki is a statuesque green eyed pink and blue blonde. She has a body like Bruce Lee and makes Miss World look like the Incredible Hulk. She is excellent in bed (given half the chance.) Her hero is Bruce Lee, who proposed to her a number of times, but who she had to turn down because she was only 10 at the time. Her heroine is Pat Benatar who hopes to be able to sing as well as Beki one day. Her ambitions include meeting Rudolph Nureyev and sailing single-handedly around his hips, and her previous occupations include six months as a sumo wrestler and two years as a gigolo."

She was also a member of Vice Squad, one of the most glorious of all the bands to explode following punk's original breakthrough. The Pistols, in fact, had already broken up by the time Vice Squad made their first move, but The Clash were making triple albums and Gen X had gone all disco trash. Vice Squad was the antidote to so much new wave horseheadery, the solution, too, to the studs and mohawks zygosity of the rest of the so-called Street Punk rebellion. And if, as Beki later insisted, the group members really did all loathe one another, the tension in the ranks never detracted from their power.

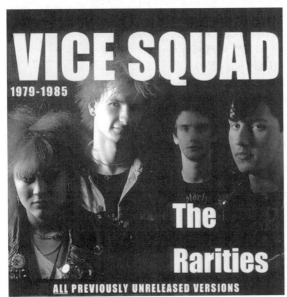

Vice Squad formed in 1979 in Bristol. Rebecca Bond was just 15 at the time, but there was never any trace of juvenile jailbait delinquency about her. A riotous mass of studs and leather, her shock of blonde hair streaked with day-glo and her voice an all- penetrating bellow, she had barely been singing for six months when she piloted Vice Squad through their debut, a screaming contribution (*Nothing*) on the seminal AVON CALLING compilation.

Her bandmates were more experienced — drummer Shane Baldwin and guitarist Dave Bateman had been playing together for at least a couple of years in makeshift bands like The Spam, The Proletariat and TV Brakes. "We played a lot of local gigs and together wrote many of the songs [which] would later be used by Vice Squad. We didn't play any big gigs or make proper recordings [some garageland demos would appear on Vice Squad's THE RARITIES collection in 1999], but it's fair to say that without TV Brakes there would never have been a Vice Squad."

Bassist Mark Hambly came aboard at the same time as Beki (second guitarist Mark Byrne followed.) In this form, Vice Squad cut their first single for their own Riot City label, the still-anthemic *Last Rockers*. A brazen call to arms and armor, the template around which most of the third wave punk sound would ultimately gravitate, *Last Rockers* tore up the independent chart and was single-handedly responsible for the vast turn-out which greeted the group's first UK tour — and the haste with which the Regal Zonophone label snapped them up.

A second Riot City release, the similarly urgent *Resurrection* followed in May 1981, backed by Bondage's animal rights anthem *Humane*. By the end of the year, Vice Squad was readying their major label debut, the album NO CAUSE FOR CONCERN. Bondage herself later professed to hate the record, but with Vice Squad now gigging constantly, there was no time for regrets or recriminations, particularly as the album shot into the Top 30.

"We had the songs and we had the energy," Bondage reflected later. "But apart from *Last Rockers*, none of the records ever captured that." That's not quite true, but when similar failings dogged STAND STRONG STAND PROUD, Vice Squad's sophomore album the following year, Bondage exercised the only option she believed was available, quitting the band in fall 1982, soon after recording one final single, *Citizen*.

Linking with ex-U.K. Subs drummer Steve Roberts, Chelsea bassist Linc and guitarist Mo Mo Sex, Bondage formed Ligotage, a truly magnificent and cruelly underrated act whose solitary single, 1983's *Crime And Passion*, captured all the lost opportunities which Vice Squad had been presented with. The remainder of that group, meanwhile, added a new vocalist, Lia, and cut a third album, SHOT AWAY, in 1984.

All faded from the scene thereafter. by 1998, however, Beki and the band had reunited, and Vice Squad was back in action, visiting the US on the Social Chaos tour and releasing a new album.

VICE SQUAD ORIGINAL DISCOGRAPHY
Singles
- *Last Rockers / Latex Love / Living On Dreams* (Riot City RIOT 1, 1981)
- *Resurrection / Young Blood / Humane* (Riot City RIOT 2, 1981)
- *Out Of Reach / So What For The 80s / Sterile* (Regal Zonophone Z26, 1982)
- *Rock'n'Roll Massacre / Stand Strong And Proud / Tomorrow* (Regal Zonophone Z30, 1982)
- *Citizen / Scarred For Life / Faceless Men* (Regal Zonophone Z34, 1982)

Albums
- NO CAUSE FOR CONCERN (Regal Zonophone ZEM 103, 1981)
- STAND STRONG STAND PROUD (Regal Zonophone ZEM 104, 1982)
- LAST ROCKERS — THE SINGLES (Abstract 805, 1992)
- BBC SESSIONS (Anagram CDPUNK 99, 1997)
- THE RARITIES (Captain Oi AHOY 123, 1999)

Last Words . . .

And at the end of the day, what did punk really accomplish?

It didn't kill the dinosaurs, nor end the mega-stadium superstars, for instead, it created new ones. The Jam played Wembley, The Clash played Madison Square, Siouxsie and the Banshees co-headlined Lollapalooza.

It did not change the record companies. In 1976, EMI signed The Sex Pistols for Europe, in 1977 Warners signed them for America. And in 1999, EMI and Warners signed each other up and merged.

And it did not change the world.

But it did create a whole new underclass, which would one day grow up to make something of itself. Everything which today, we describe as "alternative" rock owes its parentage to punk. Or, if not its parentage, its right to look elsewhere for such. It wasn't the first time in modern musical history that the slate had been wiped clean, but it was the most lasting.

Careening into the melting pot that the media called "punk" (and later adapted to New Wave, for fear of scaring away the faint-at-heart), the classic rock grind of The Clash, the Motown Mod moping of The Jam, the misogynist psychedelia of The Stranglers, the Detroit Stooge adrenaline of The Damned, the furious folk of Otway-Barrett, the rabble rousing battle cries of Sham 69, the beetle-browed poetics of Elvis Costello, the funk of The Pop Group, the pop of The Buzzcocks, and the industrial clatter of Throbbing Gristle, all were drawn in, stirred around and then spat out like bulletin bullets, to lead a whole new movement into the 80's promised land. And the fact that that promised land turned out a little less exciting than anyone expected was only the other side of the same delicious deal.

But like the clichéd old T-shirt insisted, the spirit of punk never did die. Through the oi! and hardcore holocausts of the early decade, in the underground of Orange County and the backwoods of Washington State . . . in 1992, John Lydon (Rotten as was) complained that a German journalist had asked him, seriously, why he was ripping off Nirvana. "I told him he was Very Mistaken Indeed." And the Business' Mickey Fitz, reflecting around the same time, recalled, "I remember watching Nirvana's *Smells Like Teen Spirit* on the telly and everyone said 'ah, this new grunge is great,' and I went — grunge? This is punk rock."

Close to a decade on from then, grunge is gone, Nirvana is gone, and punk itself is getting ready for its 25th anniversary party. "In 2001," The Damned's Brian James recently pointed out, "punk will have been around for as long as the Queen when the Pistols did *God Save The Queen*." And there are those who'd have you believe that it's just about as relevant as well.

They'd be wrong. Punk survived, punk has grown, punk has expanded beyond even the absurdly broad limits that marked it out in the first place. Where once there was only one Elvis Costello, today there are dozens who've learned from him and thrived. Where once there was only one Clash, today there is a world which reaches from Rancid and The Bosstones to Primal Scream and Death In Vegas. And where once there was only one localized scene, today there is an entire new generation girding their loins and distorting their amps, in readiness for the call to arms.

For punk never did accomplish any of the things that it supposedly set out to do. But it never set a time limit either.

Billy Idol, Cow Palace, San Francisco, CA 1984
copyright Phil Anderson / KAOS200 Magazine

Last Words . . .

ALSO FROM COLLECTOR'S GUIDE PUBLISHING

Be sure to watch for

Pop:
ISBN 1-896522-25-4

Glam:
ISBN 1-896522-26-2

Women In Rock:
ISBN 1-896522-29-7